THE CHRIST REVEALED

Brother Rick,
May the Grace and Peace
of our Lord Jesus Christ be with
you always.

Paul

G. PAUL ROBINSON

THE CHRIST REVEALED

Second Edition

TATE PUBLISHING
AND ENTERPRISES, LLC

The Christ Revealed
Second Edition

Published by Tate Publishing & Enterprises, LLC
127 E. Trade Center Terrace | Mustang, Oklahoma 73064 USA
1.888.361.9473 | www.tatepublishing.com

Tate Publishing is committed to excellence in the publishing industry. The company reflects the philosophy established by the founders, based on Psalm 68:11,
"The Lord gave the word and great was the company of those who published it."

Book cover design by Jan Sunday Quilaquil

Published in the United States of America

ISBN: 978-1-62563-253-1
1. Religion / Christian Ministry / General
2. Religion / Biblical Studies / Bible Study Guides
13.04.19

In memory of my mother,
L. Fay Robinson (1922 – 1997)
Who became for me and many others,
a personification of Christ's love,
sacrifice and compassion.

THE CHRIST REVEALED
teaching series.

Table of Contents

VI. MAJOR PROPHETS SERIES ____________ 184

VII. WISDOM SERIES ____________ 221

THE LENTEN SERIES ____________ 247

Introduction

THE CHRIST REVEALED. *A curious name for a series of bible studies.* Conventional wisdom suggests to us that one "Discovers" Jesus, albeit in a variety of ways, when we profess our Christian faith. Many Christians have told me that they remember the day, the time, and the very minute, that Jesus "came into their lives". Other Christians have indicated that the Christian experience is a commitment over time, a willingness and decision to live according to Christ. They do not recall any specific instance of "conversion" or spiritual "calling". *I am reminded of the experiences of two well-known evangelists: John Wesley and Billy Graham.*

Although Wesley had been a priest in the Church of England for a number of years, his spiritual experiences in the small parish in England in the 1700s were increasingly mundane and without meaningful spiritual substance. On 24 May 1738, at a Moravian meeting in Aldersgate Street, London, Wesley heard a reading of Martin Luther's preface to the Epistle to the Romans, and penned the now famous lines "I felt my heart strangely warmed"[1],He believed that it was the hand of God, Jesus the Christ, who was beckoning him to a more active spiritual ministry. Although he did not leave the Church of England, he declared a worldwide ministry, and began fervently preaching, sometimes 4-5 sermons a day.. for the next 50 years until his death. He is most remembered as the founding patriarch of the Methodist church and often spoke of a "*personal"* relationship with Jesus Christ. Perhaps in his case, he more fully "*ReDiscovered*" Jesus in the midst of his Church of England clergy vocation.

Billy Graham began his journey as the son of a dairy farmer near Charlotte, North Carolina. He attended a revival meeting in 1934 led by the evangelist Mordecai Ham, underwent a "religious" experience, and professed his decision for Christ at age 16. During his early years, he was torn between fundamentalism and modernism (*a movement that applied scholarly methods of textual and historical criticism to the study of the Bible*). He attended Bob Jones University but found it too legalistic and the rules too confining.[2] In 1937, Graham transferred to the Florida Bible Institute (now Trinity College of

---

[1] Dreyer, Frederick A. (1999). *The Genesis of Methodism*. Lehigh University Press. pg. 27.

[2] *Time, God's Billy Pulpit*, November 15, 1993

Florida). In his autobiography Graham writes that he would often take all-night walks on the Temple Terrace Golf and Country Club in Florida and *"struggle with the Holy Spirit over the call to be a minister".* He goes on to say that the *"inner, irresistible urge would not subside".*[3]

While on a spiritual retreat in 1949 in the San Bernadino mountains of southern California, he decided to set aside his intellectual doubts about Christianity and simply and boldly "preach the Gospel." He subsequently preached in barns, homes, street corners, churches and, ultimately, in the largest stadiums throughout the world and on radio and television to an estimated 2.2 billion persons. An estimated 2.5 million people responded to the powerful alter calls while "Just as I Am" was sung by the huge crusade choirs[4].

Both John Wesley and Billy Graham had an initial conversion experience, a "*Discover Jesus*" experience, when they accepted Jesus Christ as their Lord and Savior. Wesley became a priest and Graham was converted at the Mordecai Ham revival. Both men could also focus on the time and place when they began to "*ReDiscover Jesus*"; that is, they experienced a fuller, more intimate, action-oriented calling, (i.e. *A more personal relationship with Jesus Christ).* Many of us have sensed the healing touch of the Holy Spirit from Jesus Christ. We have sensed His presence and love, yet, we have willfully gone our separate ways. Again and again, we return to "ReDiscover" that presence and eternal calling of Jesus the Christ.

This book is a series of bible studies and Lenten series about the historical and spiritual savior. The man who was born in Bethlehem, grew to manhood in Nazareth, and was the Christ (Hebrew: Messiah) which means *The Anointed One*. He was the Son of God, the ***Imago Dei*** (image of God) for all mankind. Judaism, Islam, Hinduism, Buddhism and many of the world's religions have discovered Jesus, the man. They believe that He was a great prophet. Christians have initially discovered and over time, "*rediscovered*", more of Jesus: Our belief is that He was (and is) the Christ. The Messiah. The Savior of all persons on this earth.

---

[3] Billy Graham, Just As I Am, (San Francisco, Harper Collins Publishers, 1997), pg. 63
[4] en.wikipedia.org/wiki/Billy_Graham

THE CHRIST REVEALED teaching series was compiled in response to a call to ministry for all of us. We rediscover more of Jesus each day along our spiritual journey in so many ways... through our prayer, Holy Communion and the Holy Bible, to name a few... Perhaps one of the most powerful ways to a fuller "rediscovery" of Jesus Christ is through the comprehensive reading of the Old and New Testaments, including the prophets and the eye-witnesses of the resurrected Lord, the New Testament Apostles and disciples. For instance, scripture records over 500 eye-witnesses of our resurrected Lord and Savior, Jesus the Christ.

Christ's message is as powerful today as it was in the world over 2,000 years ago. His promise of unconditional love and eternal life in the face of all adversity and His powerful Grace covenant abide with us through our belief, faith, hope and commitment to Him: God the Father, Son and Holy Spirit.

There are many roads to the initial discovery and fuller "*rediscovery* " of Jesus the Christ. I have traveled the *Evangelical Episcopal* (Anglican) road... It has been said that Anglicanism is mid-way and provides a "bridge" between the Catholic and Protestant churches. In a broad sense, Evangelicalism is midway between fundamentalist and liberal thought with a focus on outreach and Holy scripture, particularly the Gospel message of the cross, atonement and resurrection of Jesus the Christ. Together, these disciplines embrace both the congregational and liturgical polities through primarily scripture, then reason and, finally, tradition.

It was my privilege to complete a Master's of Divinity degree at an Episcopal Seminary including certification as a Hospital Chaplain. My wife, Margaret, and I traveled to Europe and shared the Gospel message of the Holy Scriptures in churches and seminaries in France, Austria, Switzerland and Germany.

THE CHRIST *REVEALED* is a series of selected bible studies and Lenten series which are Christo-centric. It is taught from a "broad church" perspective. It is believed that *all* Christian churches, Anglican, Episcopal, Catholic, Eastern Orthodox, Lutheran, Baptist, Methodist, Presbyterian, Pentecostal, Nazarene, Evangelical *et al*, have a common bond in the Gospel of Jesus Christ and have something to teach us. This comprehensive and ecumenical work has been researched, edited and compiled over 5 years.

Grateful acknowledgment goes to the wealth of information gleaned from the seminary books and resources listed in each series and the internet information available from subjects referenced in www.wacriswell.com, www.en.wikipedia.org/wiki/, www.goarch.org, www.gotquestions.org, www.catholic.com, www.episcopalchurch.org, www.biblegateway.com, and www.anglicancommunion.org. For more information, please email: **_ReDiscoverJesus7@Gmail.com_** *or go online:* **_ReDiscover-Jesus.com._**

Renamed for publication in 2013: **THE CHRIST *REVEALED.***

THE SCARLET THREAD

The theme of Christ
is revealed in every book of the Old Testament.

The theme of Christ can be found throughout the holy scriptures. This subtle, yet powerful truth regarding the inspired word of God reveals to us a master's plan which began in the Old Testament Pentateuch and carried through the law and prophets.

Genesis (5)	The Seed of the woman
Exodus	The Lamb for sinners slain
Leviticus	Our High Priest
Numbers	The Star of Jacob
Deuteronomy	Prophet like Moses, Great Rock
Joshua (12)	Captain of the Lord of Hosts
Judges	The Messenger of Jehovah
Ruth	The Kinsman Redeemer
1 Samuel	The Great Judge
2 Samuel	The Princely King
1 Kings	David's choice
2 Kings	The Holiest of all
1 Chronicles	The King by birth
2 Chronicles	The King by judgment
Ezra	The Lord of Heaven and Earth
Nehemiah	The Builder
Esther	Our Mordecai
Job (5)	Risen Returning Redeemer
Psalms	Son of God, Good Shepherd
Proverbs	Our Wisdom
Ecclesiastes	The One Above the Sun
Song of Solomon	The Great Church Lover
Isaiah (5)	Suffering, Glorified Servant
Jeremiah	Lord Our Righteousness
Lamentations	The Man of Sorrows
Ezekiel	The Glorious God
Daniel	Smithing Stone, Messiah
Hosea (12)	The Risen Son of God
Joel	Out Pourer of the Spirit
Amos	The Eternal Christ
Obadiah	The Forgiving Christ
Jonah	The Risen Prophet
Micah	The Bethlehemite
Nahum	Bringer of Good Tidings
Habakkuk	Lord of His Holy Temple
Zephaniah	The Merciful Christ
Haggai	Desire of All Nations
Zechariah	The Branch
Malachi	Son of Righteousness

THE SCARLET THREAD[5]

The theme of Christ
is revealed in every book of the NewTestament.

The theme of Christ can be found throughout the holy scriptures. This subtle, yet powerful truth regarding the inspired word of God reveals to us a master's plan which continued with the Gospels, the good news of Christ, the Acts of the Apostles, the epistles of St. Paul, and the letters of St. Peter, St. John and St. James. Finally, the apocalypse was foretold in the Revelation.

Matthew (4)	The King of the Jews
Mark	The Servant
Luke	The Perfect Son of Man
John	The Son of God
Acts (1)	The Ascended Lord
Romans (14)	Lord Our Righteousness
1 Corinthians	Our Resurrection
2 Corinthians	Our Comforter
Galatians	The End of the Law
Ephesians	The Head of the Church
Philippians	The Supplier of Every Need
Colossians	The Fullness of the Godhead
1 Thessalonians	He comes for His Church
2 Thessalonians	He comes with His Church
1 Timothy	The Mediator
2 Timothy	The Bestower of Crowns
Titus	Great God and Savior
Philemon	Prayer of Crowns
Hebrews	Rest of the Faith
James (7)	The Lord Drawing Nigh
1 Peter	The Vicarious Suffere
2 Peter	The Lord of Glory
1 John	The Way
2 John	The Truth
3 John	The Life
Jude	Our Security
Revelation (1)	Lion of Judah, King of Kings, Lord of Lords.

OT Groups:		NT Groups:	
	Torah (5)		**Gospels (4)**
	Historical Books (12)		History (1)
	Wisdom Books (5)		Pauline Epistles (14)
	Major Prophets (5)		General Epistles (7)
	Minor Prophets (12)		Revelation (1)

---

[5] www.wacriswell.com/index.cfm/FuseAction/Home.Home.cfm

THE HISTORICAL JESUS

Chosen Apostles Of Jesus Christ	**Eye Witnesses to the Resurrected Jesus Christ**	**Direct Post-Resurrection Accounts of Jesus Christ**
	Mary Magdalene	
St. Peter	**St. Peter**	**St. (John) Mark** Gospel of Mark
St. James The Greater	**St. James** The Greater	
St. Matthew	**St. Matthew**	**St. Matthew** Gospel of Matthew
(St. Paul) (On Damascus Road)	**St. Paul** (On Damascus Road)	(14 Epistles) **St. Luke** Gospel of Luke Acts of the Apostles
St. Simon	**St. Simon**	**Philo** 20 – 50 AD
St. Barth'mew	**St. Barth'mew**	Greek Historian
St. Philip	**St. Philip**	
St. Thomas	**St. Thomas**	**Josephus** 37 – 100 AD
St. Andrew	**St. Andrew**	Jewish Historian
St. Jude	**St. Jude**	**Clement I** Bishop of Rome – 99AD
St. James, The Less	**St. James,** The Less	**Ignatius** Bishop of Antioch-117AD
Judas Escariot	**2 Disciples** (Road to Emmaus)	**Polycarp** Bishop of Smyrna-155AD
	Gathering of 500 (1 Corinthians 15:6)	**Ireneaus** Bishop of Lyons-202AD
St. John	**St. John**	**St. John** Gospel of John

THE CHRIST REVEALED teaching series				
	Series	Course 1	Course 2	Course 3
I	*Cornerstone* (10 weeks)	*Gospel of St. John*	*Acts of the Apostles*	*Jesus the Messiah*
II	*Synoptic Gospels* (10 weeks)	*Gospel of St. Matthew*	*Gospel of St. Mark*	*Gospel of St. Luke*
III	*Missionary* (10 weeks)	*Epistles to the Romans and Thessalonians*	*Epistles To the Corinthians*	*Prison Epistles, Galatians & the Pastoral Epistles*
IV	*Major Apostles* (8 weeks)	*Epistle to the Hebrews*	*Ltrs of St. John, James, & Peter*	*Revelation of St. John the Divine*
V	*Genesis* (12 weeks)	*Book of Genesis*	*Book of Exodus*	*Book of Deuteronomy*
VI	*Major Prophets* (12 weeks)	*Books of Isaiah & Ezekiel*	*Books of Daniel & Jeremiah*	*Book of Psalms*
VII	*Wisdom* (10 weeks)	*Book of Job*	*Book of Proverbs*	*Book of Ecclesiastes*

Group Leader & Bible Study suggestions for a well-paced, meaningful group bible study

EASY-TO-TEACH Instructions. [6]

PREPARATION:

Choose a group leader and an alternate group leader. The group can choose 1 of the 7 series (note: 3 courses each) or the 5-part (week) Lenten series. As each Bible study series is chosen, the group leader simply indicates the series in the volume and begins the bible study. *Each bible study person should have a personal bible, a pen or pencil and his or her personal copy of* **THE CHRIST *REVEALED*.** *Each session should last approximately 45-55 minutes. Groups of 10-30 study participants work best.*

FORMAT OF EACH COURSE:

Background & Summary information – Usually read at the beginning of each course by the group leader or designated person(s).

Suggested Reading Schedule and Discussion - (*assigned home weekly readings for each course*).[7] The group leader will begin each session by reading each discussion question and provided the answer at the end of each weekly reading assignment. Encourage responses and discussion from the entire group. Please n*ote : If time allows, the group leader may begin reading the next assigned 7-chapters. Some of the courses may contain multiple readings for the same week due to the shortness of the epistle or book (examples: Missionary, Major Apostles, Major Prophets series.)*

Key verses – Usually read at the end of each section by the group leader or designated person(s). This is a good time for the group to reflect on the overall course and it's relation to the Holy Bible and Christianity..

---

[6] Please note that each course of a series refers to at least one book. The exception is the ***Jesus the Messiah course*** in the ***Cornerstone series*** which includes Bible references throughout the Gospels.

[7] Please Notice:In some cases, reading assignments for a given week span more that one book due to the short length of the assignment and/or book.

I. CORNERSTONE SERIES

The Gospel of St. John, the Acts of the Apostles, and a compilation of Jesus, the Messiah.

The *Cornerstone* series is the first of the teaching series. It includes two of the most powerful books of the New Testament and *Jesus Christ the Messiah,* a powerful synopsis of Our Lord which includes His Miracles, Messianic Prophecies, Apostolic Miracles, Post-resurrection appearances, and Holy Scripture references. The *Gospel of John* is unique in that St. John gives us an understanding of the *Divinity* of Jesus. The *Book of the Acts of the Apostles* gives us a recorded history of the early church.

Course One:	**The Gospel of St. John**
Course Two:	**The Acts of the Apostles**
Course Three:	**Jesus Christ, the Messiah**

Series I. Course I
Gospel of St. John

The gospel of St. John was written by an eye-witness and apostle of Jesus, St. John "the Divine", the son of Zebedee, brother of James, called "a son of thunder", approximately A.D. 85-90

Many scholars agree that he also wrote 1st, 2nd, 3rd John and the book of Revelation. church fathers and early bishops of the church, Ignatius, Origen, Irenaeus, Pothinus, Polycarp and Theophilus credit St. John with writing the Gospel, most probably from Ephesus.

Archeological evidence (a few verses from chapter 18, Egypt, 1935) places the writing of the gospel no later than the end of the first century. It was written after the destruction of Jerusalem in 70 AD and before St. John's exile to the isle of Patmos.The so-called "Monarchian Prologue" to the fourth gospel (c. 200) supports A.D. 96 or one of the years immediately following as to the time of its writing.

Most scholars agree on a range of 90-100 AD. The gospel was already in existence early in the 2nd Century. The gospel was composed in stages (probably two or three). There is credible evidence that the gospel was written no later than the middle of the second century.

The purpose of the gospel of St. John is summarized in the words of 20:31. "These are written that you may believe that Jesus is the Christ, the son of God, and that believing you may have life in His name".

The main themes of the gospel of St. John are that Jesus Christ is God, He is Jehovah's messiah and son, and His deity is asserted many times. The gospel of St. John is somewhat different than the "Synoptic

Gospels" (St. Matthew, St. Mark and St. Luke), in that it concentrates on the deity of Christ rather than His historical presence.

St. John presents the highest Christology within the gospels. It describes Jesus as the incarnation of the divine Logos, through which all things were made, and declares him to be God. Only in the g*ospel of St. John* does Jesus talk at length about Himself and His divine role, including a substantial amount of material Jesus shared with the disciples only. Jesus' public ministry consists largely of miracles not found in the Synoptics, including raising Lazarus from the dead.

Critical scholarship in the 19th century distinguished between the 'biographical' approach of the three Synoptic Gospels and the 'theological' approach of St. John, and accordingly tended to disregard St. John as a historical source. This distinction is no longer regarded as sustainable in more recent scholarship, which emphasizes that all four gospels are both biographical and theological.

As indicated, most reference books list the date for this manuscript as 90 - 100 AD. St. John's portrayal of Jesus as the God of the Old Testament is seen most emphatically in the seven "I Am" statements of Jesus. He is the "Bread of life" (John 6:35), provided by God to feed the souls of His people, just as He provided manna from heaven to feed the Israelites in the wilderness (Exodus 16:11-36).

Jesus is the "Light of the world" (John 8:12), the same Light that God promised to His people in the Old Testament (Isaiah 30:26, 60:19-22) and which will find its culmination in the New Jerusalem when Christ the Lamb will be its Light (Revelation 21:23) and the Shepherd of Israel (Psalm 23:1, 80:1)[8]

---

[8] http://en.wikipedia.org/wiki/Gospel_of_St. John

Summary Information:[9]

Gospel of John	
Chapters:	**21**
Verses:	**879**
OT Prophecies :	**15**
Verses of Prophecy (fulfilled):	**37**
Verses of Prophecy (unfulfilled):	**7**

[9] http://en.wikipedia.org/wiki/Gospel_of_John

Course I, *Gospel of John**
Suggested Reading Schedule and Discussion:

Week 1: Chapters 1 – 7

1. What is unique about the Gospel of St. John? Why is it different than the other 3 Gospels?

___

___

___

2. How is St. John different historically than the other Apostles? What books did he write in the New Testament?

___

___

___

3. What is the first recorded miracle of Jesus Christ and why was it significant at that place and time? What were the general categories of His miracles?

___

___

___

*** Space is provided for additional notations at the end of the course.**

Course I, *Gospel of John**
Suggested Reading Schedule and Discussion:

Week 2: Chapters 8 – 14

1. Why did the Jews want to stone Jesus? Did Jesus affirm or deny the Jewish priesthood in whom in came in contact?

____

____

____

2. What is the two-fold judgment explanation of Jesus as to why He came into the World? Is His mission completed?

____

____

____

3. What powerful question of belief did Jesus pose to Martha concerning Lazarus' death? Why did Jesus tarry when He was told of Lazarus' impending death?

____

____

____

*** Space is provided for additional notations at the end of the course.**

Course I, *Gospel of John**
Suggested Reading Schedule and Discussion:

Week 3: Chapters 15 – 21

1. What is the relation that Jesus uses of the vine and the branches? Was Jesus raised in an urban or rural community?

___

___

___

2. What is the work of the Holy Spirit and what is His relationship to Jesus Christ? Discuss the Trinity.

___

___

___

3. How many times did Jesus appear to the Apostles after His resurrection? Did He appear to anyone else after His resurrection?

___

___

___

*** Space is provided for additional notations at the end of the course.**

- *In the beginning was the Word, and the Word was with God, and the Word was God...And the Word became flesh and dwelt among us, and we beheld His glory, the glory as of the only begotten of the Father, full of grace and truth" (John 1:1,14.)*

- *"For God so loved the world that He gave His only begotten Son, that whoever believes in Him should not perish but have everlasting life" (John 3:16).*

- *"Jesus said to her, 'I am the resurrection and the life. He who believes in Me, though he may die, he shall live. And whoever lives and believes in Me shall never die. Do you believe this?'" (John 11:25-26).*

- *Jesus answered, "I am the way and the truth and the life. No one comes to the Father except through me. If you really knew me, you would know my Father as well. From now on, you do know him and have seen him." (John 14:6-7).*[10]

[10] http://www.gotquestions.org/Gospel-of-John.html

The End of Course One

(Please jot down any additional notations which may be helpful in group discussions.)

Series I. Course II
Acts of the Apostles

The Acts of the Apostles was written by an eye-witness of the Apostles and disciple of Jesus, St. Luke, and the Beloved Physician. According to the early Church historian Eusebius, Luke was born at Antioch in Syria. Many scholars agree that he also wrote the Gospel of Luke. The account of the early Church was written about 63 - 64 AD. The earliest manuscript of the Luke's Gospel (*Papyrus Bodmer XIV/XV* = P^{75}), dated circa 200 AD, ascribes the work to Luke as did Irenaeus, circa 180 AD and the *Muratorian fragment* from 170 AD.

We may at most assign a probable date for the completion of the book. It is recognized by all that Acts ends abruptly. The author devotes but two verses to the two years which Paul spent at Rome. These two years were in a certain sense uneventful. Paul dwelt peaceably at Rome, and preached the kingdom of God to all who went in unto him. It seems probable that during this peaceful epoch St. Luke composed the Book of Acts and terminated it abruptly at the end of the two years, as some unrecorded vicissitude carried him out into other events.

The date of the completion of Acts is therefore dependent on the date of St. Paul's Roman captivity. Writers are quite concordant in placing the date of Paul's coming to Rome in the year 62; hence the year 64 is the most probable date for the Acts.

The authenticity of the Acts of the Apostles is proved are intrinsic evidence; The unity of style of Acts and its artistic completeness compelling us to receive the book as the work of one author. Such an effect could never arise from the piecing together bits of writings of different authors. The writer writes as an eyewitness and companion of

St. Paul.

In Acts we see the fulfillment of Christ's promises. In Acts 1:8, Jesus had declared that the Apostles should receive power when the Holy Ghost should come upon them, and should be His witnesses both in Jerusalem and in all Judea and Samaria, and unto the uttermost parts of the earth.

In John 14:12, Jesus had declared: "He that believeth in me, the works that I do, he also shall do, and greater works than these shall he does because I go to the Father".Acts tells the story of the Apostolic Age of the Early Christian church, with particular emphasis on the ministry of the Twelve Apostles and of Paul of Tarsus.

The early chapters, set in Jerusalem, discuss Jesus' Resurrection, his Ascension, the Day of Pentecost, and the start of the Twelve Apostles' ministry. The later chapters discuss Paul's conversion, his ministry, and finally his arrest and imprisonment and trip to Rome.

While St. Luke does exclude himself from those who were eyewitnesses to Jesus' ministry, he repeatedly uses the word "we" in describing the Pauline missions. Luke first joined Paul's company at Troas at about the year 51 AD and they went into Macedonia, first to Samothrace, Neapolis, and finally Philippi. Luke stayed behind to encourage the Church there.

St. Paul returned to the area on his third missionary journey seven years later. In Acts 20:5, the switch to "we" tells us that Luke has left Philippi to rejoin Paul in Troas in 58 AD where they first met. They traveled together through Miletus, Tyre, Caesarea, to Jerusalem.

Summary Information[11]:

Acts of the Apostles	
Chapters:	**28**
Verses:	**1007**
OT Prophecies:	**21**
Verses of Prophecy (fulfilled):	**14**
Verses of Prophecy (unfulfilled):	**6**

[11] http://en.wikipedia.org/wiki/Acts_of_the_Apostles

Course II, *Acts of the Apostles**
Suggested Reading Schedule and Discussion:

Week 4: Chapters 1 – 7

1. How many recorded instances were there of the "filling of the Holy Spirit" and how did they differ? Is this the same as the "Baptism of the Holy Spirit?

___

___

___

2. What happened to Ananias and Sapphira? What commandment(s) did they break?

___

___

___

3. St. Peter stated that a person must do what (actions) before he is to receive the gift of the Holy Spirit?

___

___

___

* Space is provided for additional notations at the end of the course

Course II, *Acts of the Apostles**
Suggested Reading Schedule and Discussion:

Week 5: Chapters 8 – 14

1. Who gave approval to the stoning of St. Stephen? Why was this person at the death of St. Stephen?

____

____

____

2. Where and how was St. Paul converted? Did he consider himself an Apostle equal to the others?

____

____

____

3. How did St Peter escape from prison? What did he do shortly after being released from prison?

____

____

____

* Space is provided for additional notations at the end of the course

Course II, *Acts of the Apostles**
Suggested Reading Schedule and Discussion:

Week 6: Chapters 15 – 21

1. What was discussed at the Council of Jerusalem? Did St. Peter and St. Paul agree on the final determination?

___

___

___

2. Who joined St. Paul on his missionary journeys? What famous writer(s) of the Gospels journeyed with him?

___

___

___

3. What did St. Paul say about the "unknown God"? To whom was he speaking and what was the final result?

___

___

___

* Space is provided for additional notations at the end of the course.

Course II, *Acts of the Apostles**
Suggested Reading Schedule and Discussion:

Week 7: Chapters 22 – 28

1. What was St. Paul's defense to the crowd? To what King(s) did he also defend Christianity?

____

____

____

2. What significance was St. Paul's citizenship? How did this influence his punishment and final death in Rome?

____

____

____

3. To whom did St. Paul speak regarding his faith? How did this ethnic focus influence his missionary journeys?

____

____

____

* Space is provided for additional notations at the end of the course

- *But you will receive power when the Holy Spirit comes on you; and you will be my witnesses in Jerusalem, and in all Judea and Samaria, and to the ends of the earth." (Acts 1:8)*

- *"All of them were filled with the Holy Spirit and began to speak in ...tongues as the Spirit enabled."(Acts 2:4)*

- *"But Peter and John replied, 'Judge for yourselves whether it is right in God's sight to obey you rather than God. For we cannot help speaking about what we have seen and heard.'" (Acts 4:19-20)*

- *"As he [Saul] neared Damascus on his journey, suddenly a light from heaven flashed around him. He fell to the ground and heard a voice say to him, 'Saul, Saul, why do you persecute me?' 'Who are you, Lord?' Saul asked. 'I am Jesus, whom you are persecuting,' he replied. 'Now...go into the city, and you will be told what you do.'"(Acts 9:3-6)*[12]

[12] http://www.gotquestions.org/Acts_of_the_Apostles.html

The End of Course Two

(Please jot down any additional notations which may be helpful in group discussions.)

Series I. Course III
Jesus the Messiah

During the first 12 - 63 years after Christ's death, the Apostles were prolific in their writings regarding Christ's work and the risen Lord. St. Matthew (65 AD), St. James (45 AD), Simon (renamed St. Peter) (60-65 AD) and St. John (85-96 AD), wrote first-hand, eye-witnessed accounts of Jesus the Christ

It is believed by most scholars that St. (John) Mark (63 AD) transcribed first-hand accounts of St. Peter in his Gospel of Mark, the first of the Gospels. St. Luke, the beloved gentile physician (63-64 AD) and Saul (renamed St. Paul) (54–68 AD), also wrote authoritative accounts of the early church. St. Luke and St. (John) Mark accompanied St. Paul on at least one of his three missionary journeys and the writings produced, as in the gospels, include a very descriptive and detailed account of the early church, our Lord's appearances and the apostolic miracles.

Many of the individual writings for the New Testament were completed as early as 45 AD as in the case of St. James, the half-brother of Jesus and the first bishop of Jerusalem. It is estimated that over 13,000 Syria, Latin and Greek manuscripts were copied. Over 350 copies still exist of the ancient extant manuscripts.

Approximately 365 Messianic prophecies[13] in the Old Testament as early at 1350 BC have been foretold regarding Jesus the Christ. These prophesies regarding Israel and the coming Messiah were foretold by the prophets Isaiah, Jeremiah, Ezekiel, Daniel, and the Psalmists including Moses, David and Solomon. Hundreds of fulfilled prophesies are also in the New Testament.

---

[13] www.bibleprobe.com/365messianicprophecies.htm

Although ancient mythology alludes to "gods" who were resurrected such as Dionysus, Orpheus, the virgin-born shepherd Attis, Adonis, and Mythra, Jesus Christ is the only *real* person in recorded history to predict His exact death, resurrection and, later, claim His own victory over death.

His death by crucifixion was witnessed by His Apostles, Mary Magdalene, Mary His mother, and a large number of Jews and Romans in Jerusalem. It is recorded that He appeared at least 15 times after His resurrection. Sixteen subsequent apostolic miracles are recorded through the power of the Holy Spirit and the risen Christ. Jesus Christ is recorded to have performed at least 34 miracles during His ministry on earth.

The Holy Bible has been painstakingly analyzed, translated and distributed in more countries than any other documentation in the history of mankind.

The Dead Sea scrolls, 900 in all, discovered between 1947 and 1956, reveal manuscripts dating between 150 BC and the fall of Jerusalem in 70 AD. Included are the five books of the Pentateuch, Job, the Psalms, and the Major Prophets.

.

There are some 200 names and titles of Christ found in the bible. Some of the more noteworthy names of Jesus the Christ are as follows:

- Head of the Church: (Ephesians 1:22; 4:15; 5:23)
- Holy One: (Acts 3:14; Psalm 16:10)
- King of kings and Lord of lords: (1 Timothy 6:15; Revelation 19:16)
- Prince of peace: (Isaiah 9:6)
- Son of God: (Luke 1:35; John 1:49)
- Son of man: (John 5:27)

It is noteworthy that many of these same Apostles who also witnessed Jesus' miracles and healings during His 3-year ministry on this earth, abandoned and disowned Him during the crucifixion and were left cowering in the upper room, terrified of the Jewish Sanhedrin and the Roman soldiers.

A few days later, these same "cowardly" Apostles were boldly preaching the risen Christ in Jerusalem and throughout the world as well as healing the sick and raising the dead. ***The difference: The mighty empowering of the Holy Spirit through the risen Christ.***

The 3-year historical ministry and resurrected appearances of Jesus Christ have been witnessed by literally hundreds of eye-witnesses and documented in the New Testament as well as prominent non-Christian historians: Jewish historians (ex. **Josephus**), and Greek historians (ex. **Philo**), were contemporaries of Jesus. Later, the Roman (Latin) historians (ex. **Tacitus**) documented the Christ.

The first-century Roman Tacitus, who is considered one of the more accurate historians of the ancient world, mentioned "Christians", who suffered under Pontius Pilate during the reign of Tiberius. Suetonius, chief secretary to Emperor Hadrian, wrote that there was a man named **'Christ'** who lived during the first century (***Annals* 15.44**).

Flavius Josephus is the most famous Jewish historian. In his ***Antiquities*** he refers to a **wise man named Jesus.** His conduct was good and [he] was known to be virtuous. And many people from among the Jews and the other nations became his disciples. Pilate condemned him to be crucified and to die. But those who became his disciples did not abandon his discipleship. **They reported that he had appeared to them three days after his crucifixion, and that he was alive**; accordingly he was perhaps the Messiah, concerning whom the prophets have recounted wonders."

Regarding the world's existing religions, none aspire to everlasting life through their creator. Confucius died and was buried. Buddha died and was buried. Mohammed died and was buried. Most of contemporary thought, including Humanism, Gnosticism, and so-called Spiritual "Self-fulfillment", refer to the historical Jesus as a good man.

Some religions even call Him a prophet as in the Islam Koran; however, none of the world's other religions, including contemporary Judaism, recognize the deity of Christ, the Messiah and the Savior of the world.[14]

C.S. Lewis, the famous author, former atheist and world-renowned intellectual of the 20th century, writes:[15]

> A man who was merely a man and said the sort of things Jesus said would not (only) be a great moral teacher, He would either be a lunatic--on the level with a man who says he is a poached egg—or else he would be the Devil of Hell. You must make your choice. Either this man was, and is, the son of God or else a madman or something worse. You can shut him up for a fool, you can spit on Him or kill Him as a demon; or you can fall at His feet and call Him Lord and God. But let us not come with any patronizing nonsense about His (only) being a great human teacher. He has not left that open to us.

Additional References and Peripheral Study Guides

- **John R. W. Stott, Basic Christianity, (London: Inter-Varsity Press, 2006)**
- **Alan Richardson, A Dictionary of Christian Theology, (Philadelphia: Westminster, 1976)**
- **C.S. Lewis, Mere Christianity, (New York: MacMillan Publishing, 1952)**
- **Dwight Pentecost, The Words & Works of Jesus Christ, (Grand Rapids, Zondervan,1981)**

---

[14] http://en.wikipedia.org/wiki/Jesus_the_Messiah

[15] C.S. Lewis, Mere Christianity, (New York: MacMillan Publishing, 1952, page 56)

Course III, *Jesus the Messiah**
Suggested Reading Schedule and Discussion:

Week 8: Miracles performed by Jesus Christ *(scripture references enclosed, **p35)***

1. What is unique about the life and ministry of Jesus? Does history record any other prophets, teachers or "holy men" with the same qualities and attributes?

___

___

___

2. Why did Jesus Christ perform miracles? What was the relation of His ministry to His "signs and wonders"?

___

___

___

3. Discuss the different forms of healing that Jesus Christ performed. What did the recipients have in common?

___

___

___

* Space is provided for additional notations at the end of the course.

Course III, *Jesus the Messiah**
Suggested Reading Schedule and Discussion:

Week 9: Post-Resurrection Appearances, Apostolic Miracles *(scripture references,* ***p36-37*** *)*

1. Discuss the resurrection appearances including his appearance by the "Gathering of the 500" in Galilee.

____

____

____

2. What is the "Gospel" of Jesus Christ? What relation does sin have in the Gospel or "Good News"?

____

____

____

3. To whom did Jesus Christ first appear in His resurrected state? What does this represent?

____

____

____

* Space is provided for additional notations at the end of the course

Course III, *Jesus the Messiah**

Suggested Reading Schedule and Discussion:

Week 10: Old Testament Verses of Prophecy *(scripture references enclosed.* ***p38-42*** *)*

1. Discuss some of the prophecies regarding the crucifixion of Jesus Christ. How do we know that these were historically correct?

___

___

___

2. Have all prophecies been fulfilled regarding the Christ (Messiah), and, if not, why?

___

___

___

3. Who were the major prophets and have all prophesies ceased? Who were the prophets in the book of Psalms?

___

___

___

* Space is provided for additional notations at the end of the course

Miracles performed by Jesus the Messiah

1. Water turned to wine (Cana) (John 2:6-10)
2. Nobleman's son healed (Capernaum) (John 4:46-53)
3. Draughts of fish (Sea of Galilee)
4. Demoniac in the Synagogue (Capernaum) (Matthew 12:27-30)
5. St. Peter's wife's mother healed (Capernaum) (Matthew 8:14,15)
6. Lepers cleansed (Galilee) (Matthew 8:3; Luke 17:14)
7. Paralytic healed (Capernaum) (Mark 2:3-12)
8. Healing of the cripple at Bethesda (Jerusalem) (John 5:11-15)
9. Withered hand restored (Galilee) (Matthew 12:10-13)
10. Centurion's servant healed (Capernaum) (Matthew 9:5-13)
11. Raising of the widow's son (Nain) (Luke 7:14-19)
12. Tempest stilled (Sea of Galilee) (Matthew 8:23-26; 14:32)
13. The deliverance of the demoniac of Gadara (Mark 5:7-14)
14. Healing of the woman (Capernaum) (Luke 8:43-47)
15. The raising of Jaures' daughter (Capernaum) (John 9:1-7)
16. The healing of the two blind men (Capernaum) (Matthew 9:27-30)
17. The Casting out of a dumb spirit (Capernaum) (Matthew 9:32-37)
18. The Feeding of the 5,000 (near Bethsaida) (Matthew 14:13-20)
19. Jesus walking on the sea (Sea of Galilee) (Matthew 14:25-27)
20. The healing of the daughter of woman (Phonecia) (Matthew 15:25)
21. Healing of deaf man w/ speech impediment (Decapolis) (Mark 7:32)
22. The Feeding of the 4,000 (Decapolis) (John ?? 6:21)
23. The Healing of the blind man (Bethsaida) (John 6:21)
24. The Deliverance of the Epileptic boy (Mt. Hermon) (Mark 9:26-30)
25. The Tribute money in the fish's mouth (Capernaum) (Matthew 17:27)
26. The healing of the man born blind (Jerusalem) (John 9:6-10)
27. Casting out of the blind/dumb spirit (Galilee) (Luke 11:5-20)
28. The Healing of the Woman (Perea) (Luke 13:10-15)
29. The Healing of the man w/Dropsy (Perea) (Luke 14:2-4)

30. The Raising of Lazarus from the dead (Bethany) (John 11:43-47
31. The cleansing of the ten lepers (Samaria) (Luke 17:13-20)
32. The Healing of Bartimeus (Jericho) (Mark 10:46-50)
33. The cursing of the Fig tree (Jerusalem) (Matthew 21:19)
34. The second draught of fishes (Sea of Galilee) (John 21:1-20)

Resurrection Appearances by Jesus the Messiah

1. Mary Magdalene (Mark 16:9, John 20:15-16)
2. Women at the Tomb (Matthew 28:9)
3. Two Disciples on the road to Emmaus (Luke 24:13-31)
4. St. Peter (Luke 24:34, 1 Corinthians 15:5)
5. The ten Apostles – St. Thomas absent (John 20:19)
6. The eleven Apostles – St. Thomas present (John 20:26)
7. The seven – Sts. Peter, Thomas, Nathanael, the sons of Zebedee, "others" (John 21:1-22)
8. The eleven on a mountain in Galilee (Matthew 28:16)
9. The twelve Apostles, including Matthias (1 Cor. 15:5, Acts 1:26)
10. 500 Brethren on the mountain in Galilee (1 Corinthians 15:6)
11. St. James, the Lord's brother (1 Corinthians 15:7, Galatians 1:19)
12. All of the Apostles (1 Corinthians 15:7, Mark 15:19-20, Luke 24:0-53, Acts 1:3-12, 26)
13. St. Stephen when he was stoned to death with Saul (later St. Paul) as the executioner (Acts 7:55-56)
14. St. Paul on the Damascus Road (Acts 9:3-7, 17, 27)
15. Jesus Christ's ascension (Acts 1:9)

Miracles performed by the New Testament Apostles through the power of the Holy Spirit

1. The Seventy Apostles - Various miracles (Luke 10:9,17)
2. The Apostles and St. Stephen - many miracles (Acts 2:43; 5:12, 6:8)
3. St. Philip, St. Paul and St. Barnabas -Various miracles (Acts 8:6,7,13, 14:3)

4. St. Peter:
    a. Lame man cured (Acts 3:7)
    b. Death of Ananias (Acts 5:5)
    c. Death of Sapphira (Acts 5:10)
    d. The sick healed (Acts 5:15,16)
    e. AEneas made whole (Acts 9:34)
    f. Dorcas restored to life (Acts 9:40)

5. St Paul:
    a. Elymas smitten with blindness (Acts 13:11)
    b. Lame man cured (Acts 14:10)
    c. An unclean spirit cast out (Acts 16:18)
    d. Special miracles (Acts 19:11,12)
    e. Eutychus restored to life (Acts 20:10-12)
    f. Viper's bite made harmless (Acts 28:5)
    g. Father of Publius healed (Acts 28:8)

	(30 out of 365) OT Messianic Prophecies[16] (paraphrased)	Where the prophecy appears in the Old Testament (OT), (Oral tradition from 1350 BC, Written tradition between 1150 BC and 430 B.C.)	Jesus' fulfillment of the prophecy in the NT
1	*The Messiah will be sold for 30 pieces of silver*	*And I said to them, "If it is good in your sight, give me my wages; but if not, never mind!" So they weighed out thirty shekels of silver as my wages (Zech. 11:12)*	Matthew 26:14-15
2	*The Messiah will be the offspring (descendant) of the woman (Eve)*	*And Adam called his wife's name, Eve, because she was the mother of all living (Gen. 3:20)*	Acts 3:25,26
3	*The Messiah will be a descendant of Judah*	*The scepter will not depart from Judah, or the ruler's staff from between his feet, until he comes to whom it belongs and the obedience of the nations is his. (Gen. 49:10)*	Matt. 1:2 Luke 3:33
4	*The Messiah will be a prophet like Moses*	*I will raise up for them a prophet like you from among their brothers; I will put my words in his mouth, and he will tell them everything I command him. (Dt. 18:18)*	Acts 3:22,23
5	*The Messiah will be the Son of God*	*I will proclaim the decree of the LORD He said to me, "You are my Son ; today I have become your Father. (Psa. 2:7)*	Mark 1:11 Luke 3:22 Matt. 3:17
6	*The Messiah will be raised from the dead (resurrected)*	*Because you will not abandon me to the grave, nor will you let your Holy One see decay. (Psa. 16:10)*	Luke 24:4-7 John 20:11-16 Acts 1:3, 2:32 Matt. 28:5-9 Mark 16:6

[16] www.bibleprobe.com/365messianicprophecies.htm

	(30 out of 365) OT Messianic Prophecies[17] (paraphrased)	Where the prophecy appears in the Old Testament (OT), (Oral tradition from 1350 BC, Written tradition between 1150 BC and 430 B.C.)	Jesus' fulfillment of the prophecy in the NT
7	The Messiah crucifixion experience exactly as prophesied	*You must not leave his body on the tree overnight. Be sure to bury him that same day, because anyone who is hung on a tree is under God's curse. You must not desecrate the land the LORD your God is giving you as an inheritance. (Dt. 21:23)*	Matt. 27:34-50 John 19:17-30
8	The Messiah will be sneered and mocked	*All who see me mock me; they hurl insults, shaking their heads: (Psa. 22:7)*	Luke 3:11,35-39
9	The Messiah is pierced through hands and feet	*Dogs have surrounded me; a band of evil men has encircled me, they have pierced my hands and my feet. (Psa. 22:16)* Luke 23:33,	24:36-39 John 19:18, 20:19-20,24-27
10	The Messiah's bones will not be broken	*I can count all my bones; people stare and gloat over me. (Psa. 22:17)*	John 19:31-33,36
11	Men will gamble for the Messiah's clothing	*They divide my garments among them and cast lots for my clothing. (Psa. 22:18)*	Matt. 27:35 Mark 15:24 Luke 23:34 John 19:23,24
12	The Messiah will be accused by false witnesses	*Ruthless witnesses come forward; they question me on things I know nothing about. (Psa. 35:11)*	Matt. 26:59,60 Mark 14:56,57

[17] www.bibleprobe.com/365messianicprophecies.htm

	(30 out of 365) OT Messianic Prophecies[18] (paraphrased)	Where the prophecy appears in the Old Testament (OT), (Oral tradition from 1350 BC, Written tradition between 1150 BC and 430 B.C.)	Jesus' fulfillment of the prophecy in the NT
13	The Messiah will be betrayed by a friend	*Even my close friend, whom I trusted, he who shared my bread, has lifted up his heel against me. (Psa. 41:9)*	John 13:18,21
14	The Messiah will ascend to heaven (at the right hand of God)	*When you ascended on high, you led captives in your train; you received gifts from men, even from the rebellious— that you, O LORD God, might dwell there. (Psa. 68:18)* Luke 24:51	Acts 1:9; 2:33-35, 3:20-21, 5:31,32; 7:55-56
15	The Messiah will be given vinegar and gall to drink	*They put gall in my food and gave me vinegar for my thirst. (Psa. 69:21)* Matt. 27:34	Mark 15:23 John 19:29,30
16	Great kings will pay homage and tribute to the Messiah	*The kings of Tarshish and of distant shores will bring tribute to him; the kings of Sheba and Seba will present him gifts. (Psa. 72:10)*	Matt. 2:1-11
17	The Messiah, the "stone the builders rejected" is the "head cornerstone"	*So this is what the Sovereign LORD says: See, I lay a stone in Zion, ...a precious cornerstone for a sure foundation; the one that trusts will never be dismayed. (Psa. 118:22, Isa. 28:16)*	Matt. 21:42,43 Acts 4:11 Eph. 2:20 1 Peter 2:6-8
18	The Messiah will be a descendant of David	*The days are coming, declares the LORD, when I will raise up to David a righteous Branch, a King who will reign wisely and do what is just and right in the land. (Psa. 132:11, Jer. 23:5)*	Luke 1:32,33

[18] www.bibleprobe.com/365messianicprophecies.htm

	(30 out of 365) OT Messianic Prophecies[19] (paraphrased)	Where the prophecy appears in the Old Testament (OT), (Oral tradition from 1350 BC, Written tradition between 1150 BC and 430 B.C.)	Jesus' fulfillment of the prophecy in the NT
19	The Messiah will suffer and be rejected	*He was despised and rejected by men, a man of sorrows, and familiar with suffering. Like one from whom men hide their faces he was despised, and we esteemed him not. (Isa. 53:3)*	Matt. 27:20-25 Mark 15:8-14 Luke 23:18-23 John 19:14,15
20	The Messiah's first spiritual work will be in Galilee	*Nevertheless, there will be no more gloom for those who were in distress. In the past he humbled the land of Zebulon and the land of Naphtali, but in the future he will honor Galilee of the Gentiles, by the way of the sea, along the Jordan- (Isa. 9:1)*	Matt. 4:12-16
21	The Messiah will make the blind see and the deaf hear	*Then will the eyes of the blind be opened and the ears of the deaf unstopped. (Isa. 35:5)*	Matt. 11:3-6 John 11:47
22	The Messiah will be beaten, mocked, and spat upon without resistance	*I offered my back to those who beat me, my cheeks to those who pulled out my beard; I did not hide my face from mocking and spitting. (Isa. 50:6)*	Matt. 26:67, 27:26-31
23	The Messiah will be "lifted up" and exalted.	*See, my servant will act wisely he will be raised and lifted up and highly exalted. (Isa. 52:13)*	Matthew, Mark, Luke, John
24	The Messiah will be a born of a virgin (Hebrew bible: young maiden)	*Therefore the Lord himself will give you a sign: The virgin (Hebrew bible: young maiden) will be with child and will give birth to a son, and will call him Immanuel. (Isa. 7:14)*	Matt. 1:18-25 Luke 1:26-35

[19] www.bibleprobe.com/365messianicprophecies.htm

	(30 out of 365) OT Messianic Prophecies[20] (paraphrased)	Where the prophecy appears in the Old Testament (OT), (Oral tradition from 1350 BC, Written tradition between 1150 BC and 430 B.C.)	Jesus' fulfillment of the prophecy in the NT
26	The Messiah will be pierced, beaten and killed, yet He healed us	*But he was pierced for our transgressions, he was crushed for our iniquities; the punishment that brought us peace was upon him, and by his wounds we are healed. (Isa. 53:5)*	Mark 15:37-39 Luke 23:46 John 19:30 Matt. 27:50
27	The Messiah will be silent in front of his accusers	*He was oppressed and afflicted, yet he did not open his mouth; he was led like a lamb to the slaughter, and as a sheep before her shearers is silent, so he did not open his mouth. (Isa. 53:7)*	Matt. 26:62,63, 27:12-14
28	The Messiah will be buried with the rich	*He was assigned a grave with the wicked, and with the rich in his death, though he had done no violence, nor was any deceit in his mouth.(Isa. 53:9)*	Matt. 27:59,60 Mark 15:46 Luke 23:5 John 19:38
29	The Messiah will be pierced, beaten and killed, yet He healed us	*But he was pierced for our transgressions, he was crushed for our iniquities; the punishment that brought us peace was upon him, and by his wounds we are healed. (Isa. 53:5)*	Mark 15:37-39 Luke 23:46 John 19:30 Matt. 27:50
30	The Messiah will be silent in front of his accusers	*He was oppressed and afflicted, yet he did not open his mouth; he was led like a lamb to the slaughter, and as a sheep before her shearers is silent, so he did not open his mouth. (Isa. 53:7)*	Matt. 26:62,63, 27:12-14

[20] www.bibleprobe.com/365messianicprophecies.htm

The End of Course Three

(Please jot down any additional notations which may be helpful in group discussions.)

II. SYNOPTIC GOSPELS SERIES

The three historical Gospels
of our Lord Jesus Christ
written by St. Matthew, St. Mark and St. Luke.

Rather than focus on the Divinity of Christ as in the Gospel according to St. John, The Synoptic Gospels (Saints Matthew, Mark, and Luke) focus more on the historical Jesus, His ministry, miracles and healing message to a lost world. Each gospel records our Lord's resurrection.

Course One: The Gospel of St. Matthew

Course Two: The Gospel of St. Mark

Course Three: The Gospel of St. Luke

Series II. Course I
Gospel of Matthew

Matthew the Evangelist (מתי/מתתיהו, "Gift of Yahweh", Standard Hebrew and Tiberian Hebrew: *Mattay* or *Mattithyahu*; Septuagint Greek: Ματθαῖος, *Matthaios*) was, according to Christian tradition, one of the twelve Apostles of Jesus and one of the four Evangelists.

Among the early followers and apostles of Jesus, Matthew is mentioned in Mt 9:9 and Mt 10:3 as a former tax collector from Capernaum who was called into the circle of the Twelve by Jesus. He is also named among the number of the Twelve, but without identification of his background, in Mk 3:18, Lk 6:15 and Acts 1:13. He is called Levi, son of Alpheus, in Mk 2:14 and Lk 5:27. He may have collected taxes from the Hebrew people for Herod Antipas. Matthew was called by Jesus of Nazareth to be one of the Twelve Disciples. According to the New Testament he was one of the witnesses of the Resurrection and the Ascension.[21]

The Early Christian tradition attributes the Gospel to Matthew, one of Jesus' disciples; The first evidence for Matthean authorship was believed to be Papias, a second century Bishop of Hierapolis. His findings are stated in Eusebius H.E. 3.39, that says, 'Matthew made and ordered arrangement of the oracles in the Hebrew (or: Aramaic) language, and each one translated it as he was able'. A Roman tax collector such as Matthew would have been detailed.

Some scholars believe that the Gospel was originally composed in Greek rather than being a translation from Aramaic or Hebrew. Matthew's birth narrative, with the homage of the Wise Men, the flight into Egypt and the massacre of the innocents, has no parallel in other gospels and is different from Luke's corresponding account.

---

[21] http://en.wikipedia.org/wiki/Saint_Matthew

Matthew was a 1st century Galilean (presumably born in Galilee, which was not part of Judea or the Roman Iudaea province) and the son of Alpheus.[5] During the Roman occupation (which began in 63 BC with the conquest of Pompey), Matthew collected taxes from the Hebrew people for Herod Antipas, the tetrarch of Galilee. His tax office was located in Capernaum. Jews who became rich in such a fashion were despised and considered outcasts. However, as a tax collector he would have been literate in Aramaic and Greek

It was in this setting, near what is today Almagor, that Jesus called Matthew to be one of the Twelve Disciples. After his call, Matthew invited Jesus home for a feast. On seeing this, the Scribes and the Pharisees criticized Jesus for eating with tax collectors and sinners. This prompted Jesus to answer, "I came not to call the righteous, but sinners" (Mark 2:17).[22]

Summary Information:

Gospel of Matthew

Chapters:	**28**
Verses:	**1071**
OT Prophecies):	**25**
Verses of Prophecy (fulfilled):	**92**
Verses of Prophecy (unfulfilled):	**164**

Additional References and Peripheral Study Guides

- **Burton Throckmorton, Jr. Gospel Parallels, (Nashville, Thomas Nelson Publishers, 1979)**
- **Pope John Paul II, Crossing the Threshold of Hope, (New York, Alfred A. Knopf, 1994)**
- **J. Dwight Pentecost, The Words & Works of Jesus Christ, (Grand Rapids, Zondervan,1981)**
- **Kenneth Scott LaTourette, A History of Christianity, Vol. 1, (New York, Harper & Row, 1975)**

---

22 http://en.wikipedia.org/wiki/Gospel_of_St. Matthew

Course I, *Gospel of Matthew**
Suggested Reading Schedule and Discussion:

Week 1: Chapters 1 – 7

1. What was John the Baptist's "mission"? Did he accomplish what he was told to do?

____

____

____

2. Read and discuss the Beautitudes. What was the context of this beautiful litany of Christianity?

____

____

____

3. What was Jesus Christ's relation to the Law? Did he come to replace or destroy the laws of Moses?

____

____

____

* Space is provided for additional notations at the end of the course.

Course I, *Gospel of Matthew**
Suggested Reading Schedule and Discussion:

Week 2: Chapters 8 – 14

1. Discuss the various healings in these passages. What was common in all of the miraculous healings?

____

____

____

2. Name the twelve Apostles that Jesus chose. How many of these were martyred or committed suicide?

____

____

____

3. Discuss the parables in these passages. Why did Jesus teach in parables?

____

____

____

* Space is provided for additional notations at the end of the course.

Course I, *Gospel of Matthew**
Suggested Reading Schedule and Discussion:

Week 3: Chapters 15 – 21

1. What was the Transfiguration? Who were Apostles present and who did they see?

___

___

___

2. What did Jesus mean when He said, "Some of you here will not taste death before they see the Son of Man coming in His kingdom"?

___

___

___

3. When Christ asked, "Who do the people say the Son of Man is?" and what was St. Peter's reply?

___

___

___

* Space is provided for additional notations at the end of the course.

Course I, *Gospel of Matthew**
Suggested Reading Schedule and Discussion:

Week 4: Chapters 21– 28

1. What is the state of marriage at the resurrection? How does this differ in Mormonism and related religions?

___

___

___

2. What are the greatest commandments? What relation do these have with the 10 commandments of Moses?

___

___

___

3. What was Christ's analogy of the fig tree? What other examples in his parables of natural harvesting and crops come to mind?

___

___

___

* Space is provided for additional notations at the end of the course

- *"Do not think that I have come to abolish the Law or the Prophets; I have not come to abolish them but to fulfill them." (Matthew 5:17).*

- *"This, then, is how you should pray: 'Our Father in heaven, hallowed be your name, your kingdom come, your will be done on earth as it is in heaven. Give us today our daily bread. Forgive us our debts, as we also have forgiven our debtors. And lead us not into temptation, but deliver us from the evil one." (Matthew 6:9-13).*

- *"What good will it be for a man if he gains the whole world, yet forfeits his soul? Or what can a man give in exchange for his soul?" (Matthew 16:26).*

- *"Jesus replied: "'Love the Lord your God with all your heart and with all your soul and with all your mind.'...And the second is like it: 'Love your neighbor as yourself.' All the Law and the Prophets hang on these two." Matthew 22:37-40*

The End of Course One

(Please jot down any additional notations which may be helpful in group discussions.)

Series II. Course II
Gospel of Mark

Although the Gospel of Mark does not explicitly name its author, it is the unanimous testimony of early church fathers that St. (John) Mark was the author. He was an associate of the Apostle St. Peter, and evidently his spiritual son (1 Peter 5:13). From St. Peter he received first-hand information of the events and teachings of the Lord, and preserved the information in written form.

It is also generally agreed that St. Mark is the John Mark of the New Testament (Acts 12:12). His mother was a wealthy and prominent Christian in the Jerusalem church, and probably the church met in her home.

St. Mark joined St. Paul and St. Barnabas on their first missionary journey, but not on the second because of a strong disagreement between the two men (Acts 15:37-38). However, near the end of St. Paul's life he called for St. Mark to be with him (2 Timothy 4:11). Irenaeus concurred with this tradition, as did Origen of Alexandria, Tertullian, and others.

Irenaeus, Bishop of Lyons, wrote in the second half of the second century, that the four Gospels were to be accepted as written. As a youth, he had been a pupil of Polycarp, Bishop of Smyrna, who had talked to the Apostles. Later, the Bishop of Alexandria, Athanasius, accepted all 27 canonized books of the New Testament in 367 AD.

Following Augustine of Hippo, the gospel of Mark was traditionally believed by Christian churches to be based on the Gospel of Matthew, an epitome, and accordingly, it is placed after that gospel in most

Bibles. However, most contemporary scholars regard it as the earliest of the canonical gospels (*c* 70 AD). According to the two-source hypothesis, it was one source for material in the other synoptic gospels, Matthew and Luke.

Clement of Alexandria, writing at the end of the 2nd century, also reported an ancient tradition that Mark was urged by those who had heard Peter's speeches in Rome to write what the Apostle had said. Scholars have generally attributed the location as Rome.

Mark is the shortest canonical gospel. Manuscripts, both scrolls and codices, tend to lose text at the beginning and the end, not unlike a coverless paperback in a backpack. These losses are characteristically unconnected with excisions. For instance, Mark 1:1 has been found in two different forms.

Most manuscripts of Mark, including the 4th-century Codex Vaticanus, have the text "son of God", but three important manuscripts do not. Those three are: Codex Sinaiticus (01, א; dated 4th century), Codex Koridethi (038, Θ; 9th century), and the text called Minuscule 28(11th century).

Starting in the 19th century, textual critics have commonly asserted that Mark 16:9–20, describing some disciples' encounters with the resurrected Jesus, was a later addition to the gospel.

Mark 16:8 stops at the empty tomb without further explanation. The last twelve verses are missing from the oldest manuscripts of Mark's Gospel. The style of these verses differs from the rest of Mark, suggesting they were a later addition.

In a handful of manuscripts, a "short ending" is included after 16:8, but before the "long ending", and exists by itself in one of the earliest Old

Latin codices, Codex Bobiensis. By the 5th century, at least four different endings have been attested. Most likely, the Long Ending (16:9-20) started as a summary of evidence for Jesus' resurrection and the apostles' divine mission, based on other gospels.

The gospel narrates the life of Jesus of Nazareth from his baptism by John the Baptist to the resurrection, but it concentrates particularly on the last week of his life (chapters 11-16, the trip to Jerusalem). It calls him the Son of Man, the Son of God, and the Christ (the Greek translation of Messiah).[23]

Summary Information:

Gospel of Mark	
Chapters:	**16**
Verses:	**678**
OT Prophecies :	**11**
Verses of Prophecy (fulfilled):	**43**
Verses of Prophecy (unfulfilled):	**53**

[23] http://en.wikipedia.org/wiki/Gospel_of_St. Mark

Course II, *Gospel of Mark**

Suggested Reading Schedule and Discussion:

Week 5: Chapters 1 – 7

1. Who did Jesus say was His mother, brothers and sister? Did Jesus ever name his father and/or mother?

___

___

___

2. How did Jesus send out the 12 disciples and for what purpose? What curse would he put upon those towns that did not receive them?

___

___

___

3. Discuss some parables in these passages. Do these parables have a common theme?

___

___

___

* Space is provided for additional notations at the end of the course..

Course II, *Gospel of Mark**
Suggested Reading Schedule and Discussion:

Week 6: Chapters 8 – 16

1. What happened when Jesus tried to feed 4,000 people? What was the reaction from His disciples? Is there a similar passage in scripture?

___

___

___

2. What did Jesus say about Divorce? Was He is favor or against divorce and why?

___

___

___

3. What are the Signs of the End of the Age? Where are we in the timeline according to the signs? What can we do in preparation?

___

___

___

* Space is provided for additional notations at the end of the course..

- *And a voice came from heaven: 'You are my Son, whom I love; with you I am well pleased.'" (Mark 1:11).*

- *"Love the Lord your God will all your heart and with all your soul and with all your mind and with all your strength.' The second is this: 'Love your neighbor as yourself."(Mark 12:33).*

- *"I tell you the truth, anyone who will not receive the kingdom of God like a little child will never enter it." (Mark 10:14-15).*

- *"For even the Son of Man did not come to be served, but to serve, and to give His life as a ransom for many."(Mark 10:45).*

- *... "You are looking for Jesus the Nazarene, who was crucified. He has risen! He is not here. See the place where they laid him. But go, tell his disciples and Peter, 'He is going ahead of you into Galilee. There you will see him, just as he told you.'(Mark 16:4-7).*[24]

[24] http://www.gotquestions.org/Gospel-of-Mark.html

The End of Course Two

(Please jot down any additional notations which may be helpful in group discussions.)

Series II. Course III
Gospel of Luke

Early tradition, witnessed by the Muratorian Canon, Irenaeus (170 AD), Clement of Alexandria, Origen, and Tertullian, held that the Gospel of Luke and the Acts of the Apostles were both written by Luke, a companion of Paul.

The oldest manuscript of the gospel (200 AD) carries the attribution "the Gospel according to Luke". The Gospel of Luke and the Acts of the Apostles were written by the same author. The most direct evidence comes from the prefaces of each book. Arguments for a date between 37 AD and 61 AD for the Gospel note that Luke is addressed to "Most Excellent Theophilus," possibly a reference to the Roman-imposed High Priest of Israel between 37 AD and 41 AD, Theophilus ben Ananus. This reference would date the original copy of Luke to within 4 to 8 years after the death of Jesus.

The traditional view is that Luke, who was not an eye-witness of Jesus' ministry, wrote this after gathering the best sources of information within his reach (Luke 1:1-4). Critical scholarship generally holds to the two-source hypothesis as most probable, which argues that the author used the Gospel of Mark and the hypothetical Q document in addition to unique material, as sources for the gospel.

As with the other two synoptic gospels—Matthew and Mark—this book's purpose is to reveal the Lord Jesus Christ and all He "began to do and to teach until the day he was taken up to heaven" (Acts 1:1-2). Luke's gospel is unique in that is a meticulous history—an "orderly account" (Luke 1:3) consistent with the Luke's medical mind—often giving details the other accounts omit. Luke's history of the life of the Great Physician emphasizes His ministry to—and compassion for—Gentiles, Samaritans, women, children, tax collectors, sinners, and others regarded as outcasts in Israel.

Jesus leads a ministry of preaching, exorcism, and miracles in Galilee. His divine nature is revealed to chosen disciples at the Transfiguration, after which he and his disciples travel to Jerusalem, where he stolidly accepts crucifixion according to divine plan. The resurrected Jesus appears to his disciples on Sunday and ascends bodily to heaven.

Supposedly, this gospel recorded many sayings of Jesus but included almost no narrative content. Luke and Matthew both add these sayings to the narrative provided by Mark.

The author of Luke is usually agreed to be more faithful to the wording and order of the Q material than was the author of Matthew. In addition, Luke's versions of Jesus' more difficult or extraordinary sayings from Q are often more authentic than the same sayings in Matthew, where they have been softened. For example, in Luke, Jesus says that the poor are blessed, whereas Matthew reinterprets this paradoxical saying so that it is the poor in spirit who are blessed.

The text narrates the life of Jesus of Nazareth. The gospel opens with the miraculous births of John the Baptist and of Jesus. Jesus, born to the Virgin Mary, has a humble birth in a stable, and is attended by shepherds.

Like Mark (but unlike Matthew), the audience is Gentile, and it assures readers that Christianity is an international religion, not an exclusively Jewish sect. Luke portrays his subject in a positive light regarding Roman authorities. For example, the Jews are said to be responsible for Jesus' crucifixion, with Pontius Pilate finding no wrong.

Comparisons have been made between the annunciation narratives in Luke's Gospel with the Dead Sea scrolls manuscript Q4Q246:[25]

> "He will be great, and will be called the Son of the Most High ... The power of the Most High will overshadow you; therefore the child to be born will be called holy, the Son of God" (Luke 1:32, 35). "[X] shall be great upon the earth. [O king, all (people) shall] make [peace], and all shall serve [him. He shall be called the son of] the [G]reat [God], and by his name shall he be hailed (as) the Son of God, and they shall call him Son of the Most High."

Summary Information:

Gospel of Luke	
Chapters:	**24**
Verses:	**1151**
OT Prophecies :	**9**
Verses of Prophecy (fulfilled):	**118**
Verses of Prophecy (unfulfilled):	**103**

[25] http://en.wikipedia.org/wiki/Gospel_of_St. Luke

Course III, *Gospel of Luke**
Suggested Reading Schedule and Discussion:

Week 7: Chapters 1 – 7

1. Who was St. Luke and what relation did he have with St. Paul? What are the famous "we" passages?

___

___

___

2. How was the baby Jesus presented at the Temple? Did anyone recognize Him as the Messiah?

___

___

___

3. Contrast John the Baptist and Jesus the Christ. Were they related and how did their ministries connect?

___

___

___

* Space is provided for additional notations at the end of the course.

Course III, *Gospel of Luke**

Suggested Reading Schedule and Discussion:

Week 8: Chapters 8 – 14

1. What was Peter's confession of Christ? Did he always confess Christ as the Messiah?

___

___

___

2. Describe Jesus "sending out the 72". What relation did these disciples have with the 12 Apostles?

___

___

___

3. What did Jesus have to say about prayer? Did He say how we are to pray? Should we pray to God or Jesus?

___

___

___

* Space is provided for additional notations at the end of the course.

Course III, *Gospel of Luke**
Suggested Reading Schedule and Discussion:

Week 9: Chapters 15 – 21

1. Describe the parables of the lost sheep and son. Do these parables haves something in common?

____

____

____

2. How does Jesus describe the Coming of the Kingdom? How does that relate to the "second coming"?

____

____

____

3. Describe the parable of the rich young ruler. Does this mean that we are supposed to give everything to God?

____

____

____

* Space is provided for additional notations at the end of the course.

Course III, *Gospel of Luke**
Suggested Reading Schedule and Discussion:

Week 10: Chapters 22– 24

1. Describe the Last Supper. What were His admonitions to His disciples and followers of Christ?

___

___

___

2. What happened on the road to Emmaus? When did he men recognize Jesus? How is this possible?

___

___

___

3. Who buried Jesus and why was it hurried? Were the preparations complete or was a return visit necessary?

___

___

___

* Space is provided for additional notations at the end of the course.

- *John answered them all, 'I baptize you with water. But one more powerful than I will come, the thongs of whose sandals I am not worthy to untie. He will baptize you with the Holy Spirit and with fire.'" (Luke 3:16)*

- *"'The Spirit of the Lord is on me, because he has anointed me to preach good news to the poor. He has sent me to proclaim freedom for the prisoners and recovery of sight for the blind, to release the oppressed, to proclaim the year of the Lord's favor.' Today this scripture is fulfilled in your hearing." (Luke 4:18-21).*

- *When they came to the place called the Skull, there they crucified him, along with the criminals—one on his right, the other on his left. Jesus said, 'Father, forgive them, for they do not know what they are doing.'" (Luke 23:33-34)."*

- *"On the first day of the week, very early in the morning, the women took the spices…They found the stone rolled away from the tomb, but when they entered, they did not find the body of the Lord Jesus." Luke 24:1-3*[26]

[26] http://www.gotquestions.org/Gospel-of-Luke.html

Most Scholars agree that a number of passages found in the earliest Gospel of St. Mark were also copied into the Gospels of Matthew and Luke (***note bold passages in St. Mark and similar text in the other Synoptic Gospels***)[27]

St. Mark	St. Matthew	St. Luke
Baptism of Jesus	Birth of Jesus	Birth of John the Baptist
Temptation	Visit of Magi	Birth, Childhood of Jesus
Beginning of Ministry	Flight to Egypt	**Baptism of Jesus**
Calling Disciples	Sermon on the Mount	Sermon on the Plain
Healing Controversy	**Baptism of Jesus**	**Temptation**
Calling the Twelve	Discipleship	**Beginning of Ministry**
Parables	**Temptation**	Healing and Teaching
Stilling of the Storm	**Beginning of Ministry**	**Calling Disciples**
Exorcism	John the Baptist	**Calling the Twelve**
Raising the Dead	**Calling Disciples**	Parable: Good Samaritan
	Healing Controversy	The Seventy
	Parables	**Parables**
	Calling the Twelve	

27 Burton Throckmorton, ED, Gospel Parallels, (Nashville, Thomas Nelson Publishers, 1979)

St. Mark

Mission of the Twelve

Trip to Phoenicia

Peter calls Jesus the Messiah

Mission of the Twelve

Transfiguration

Trip to Judea

Entrance to Jerusalem

Teaching in Temple

Last Supper, Arrest Trial

Pilate, Crucifixion

Resurrection Appearances

St. Matthew

Trip to Phoenicia

Warning re: Hypocrisy

Trip to Judea

Entrance to Jerusalem

The End Times

Teaching in Temple

End Prophecies

Last Supper, Arrest Trial

Pilate, Crucifixion

Resurrection Appearances

St. Luke

Prayer, Beelzebub

Wealth & Greed

Stilling of the Storm

Kingdom of God

Lament for Jerusalem

Faithfulness, Forgiveness

Exorcism

Peter calls Jesus Messiah

Prodigal Son

Lost & Found Parable

Transfiguration

Entrance to Jerusalem

Last Supper, Arrest Trial

Pilate, Crucifixion

Resurrection Appearances

The End of Course Three

(Please jot down any additional notations which may be helpful in group discussions.)

III. MISSIONARY SERIES

St. Paul's three missionary journeys

St. Paul was truly an anomaly in the early church. His hatred for 'The Way' was turned into one of the most inspiring witnesses of our Lord. His three missionary journeys produced prolific writings, including his powerful Epistle to the Romans. St. Paul "planted" many churches during his ministry to the Jew and, primarily, the Gentile.

Course One:	**The Epistle of St. Paul to the Romans** **The Epistles of St. Paul to the Thessalonians**
Course Two:	**The Epistles to the Corinthians**
Course Three:	**The "Prison" Epistles of St. Paul** **The Epistle of St. Paul to the Galatians** **The "Pastoral" Epistles of St. Paul**

Series III. Course I
Epistle to the Romans

St. Paul argued that faith in Christ made the Torah essentially unnecessary for salvation, exalted the Christian church as the body of Christ, and depicted the world outside the Church as under judgment. Augustine's foundational work on the Gospel as a gift (grace), on morality as life in the Spirit, on predestination, and on original sin all derives from St. Paul, especially Romans.

Thirteen epistles (and possibly Hebrews) in the New Testament are attributed to St. Paul. Critical scholars regard St. Paul's epistles (written 54-68 AD) to be among the earliest written books of the New Testament, being referenced as early as Clement of Rome (96 AD). Romans was probably written from Corinth during St. Paul's third missionary journey. It was written while preparing for Jerusalem

Chronological Table of the historical St. Paul:

St. Paul's Date of Birth approx.	**3 AD**
Christ's Crucifixion	**30 AD**
St. Paul's conversion on the Damascus road	**32 AD**
Meeting with Sergius Paulus, Proconsul of Cyprus	**46 AD**
Apostolic Assembly with Peter, James, other Apostles	**(48-49) AD**
St. Paul in Corinth	**Winter of 49-50 – Summer of 51 AD**
St. Paul in Ephesus, Meeting with Gallio, Proconsul	**(52-55) AD**
Last stay in Macedonia and Achaia	**winter of (55-56) AD**
Journey to Jerusalem and arrest	**spring of 56 AD**
Prisoner in Rome, addresses Felix, Festus, King Agrippa	**8 AD**
2 year Imprisonment in Rome	**(58-60) AD**
Approximate dating of the Martyrdom in Rome	**(67-68) AD**

The Book of Romans is primarily a work of doctrine and can be divided into four sections:

1. righteousness needed, 1:18–3:20;
2. righteousness provided, 3:21–8:39;
3. righteousness vindicated, 9:1–11:36;
4. righteousness practiced, 12:1–15:13.

For ten years before writing the letter (approx. 57 AD), St. Paul had traveled around the territories bordering the Aegean Sea evangelizing. Churches had been planted in the Roman provinces of Galatia, Macedonia, Achaia and Asia.

Paul, considering his task complete, wanted to preach the gospel in Spain, where he would not 'build upon another man's foundation'. This allowed him to visit Rome on the way, an ambition of his for a long time.

The letter to the Romans, in part, prepares them and gives reasons for his visit. With the coming of Paul to Rome the gospel was brought from the Jewish capital of Jerusalem in the east to the Gentile capital of the world in Rome in the west. The Lord himself had told Paul, "Take courage! For as you have testified things about me in Jerusalem, so you must also testify in Rome" (Acts 23:11).

The epistle to the Romans was key for the reformers. Martin Luther expressed St. Paul's doctrine of faith most strongly as justification by faith alone. John Calvin developed Augustine's predestination into double predestination. Karl Barth's commentary on the Letter to the Romans had a political as well as theological impact.

According to Jesuit scholar Joseph Fitzmyer, the book, "overwhelms the reader by the density and sublimity of the topic with which it deals, the gospel of the justification and salvation of Jew and Greek alike by the grace of God through faith in Jesus Christ, revealing the uprightness and love of God the father.

N. T. Wright notes that Romans is neither a systematic theology nor a summary of Paul's lifework, but it is by common consent his masterpiece. It dwarfs most of his other writings, an Alpine peak towering over hills and villages. Not all onlookers have viewed it in the same light or from the same angle, and their snapshots and paintings of it are sometimes remarkably unalike. Not all climbers have taken the same route up its sheer sides, and there is frequent disagreement on the best approach. What nobody doubts is that we are here dealing with a work of massive substance, presenting a formidable intellectual challenge while offering a breathtaking theological and spiritual vision[28].

Summary Information:

Epistle to the Romans	
Chapter	**16**
Verses:	**433**
OT Prophecies :	**19**
Verses of Prophecy (fulfilled):	**29**
Verses of Prophecy (unfulfilled):	**16**

Additional References and Peripheral Study Guides

- **Gunther Bornkamm, Paulus, (New York: Harper & Row Publishers, 1971)**
- **C.K.Barrett, A Commentary on the Epistle to the Romans , (New York: Harper & Row, 1971)**
- **F.F.Bruce, Paul, Apostle of the Heart Set Free, (Grand Rapids, Eerdmans Publishing, 1977)**
- **C.K.Barrett, The First Epistle to the Corinthians, (New York: Harper & Row, 1968)**

[28] http://en.wikipedia.org/wiki/Epistle_to_the_Romans

Course I, *Epistle to the Romans**
Suggested Reading Schedule and Discussion:

Week 1: Chapters 1 – 7

1. Why is Romans one of St. Paul's most important works? What are his statements on salvation?

____

____

____

2. What does St. Paul say about sexual impurity? What relation does this immoral behavior have on the soul?

____

____

____

3. What does St. Paul mean when he says, "God does not show favoritism? Contrast that with the Jewish theology of "God's chosen people".

____

____

____

* Space is provided for additional notations at the end of the course

Course I, *Epistle to the Romans**
Suggested Reading Schedule and Discussion:

Week 2: Chapters 8 - 14

1. Read Romans 8:28-39 out loud and discuss. Does God ever separate Himself from us?

___

___

___

2. Who is the remnant of Israel? What relevance, if any, does this have with Christian theology?

___

___

___

3. Where does Faith come from and what is the relation to God's Grace? Can we have Faith apart from Grace?

___

___

___

* Space is provided for additional notations at the end of the course

Course I, *Epistle to the Romans**
Suggested Reading Schedule and Discussion:

Week 3: Chapters 15 - 16

1. Why was St. Paul a minister to the Gentiles? Contrast that ministry with the ministries of St. Peter and others.

____

____

____

2. What had to be done before St. Paul could go to Rome? What other famous Apostle was martyred in Rome?

____

____

____

3. What advice did St. Paul give against those who would cause divisions? How does that relate to Christian denominations and other religions not of Christ?

____

____

____

* Space is provided for additional notations at the end of the course.

- *"For the wages of sin is death, but the gift of God is eternal life in Christ Jesus our Lord."*(Romans 6:23).

- *"And we know that in all things God works for the good of those who love him, who have been called according to his purpose."*(Romans 8:28).

- *"Who can separate us from the love of Christ? Shall tribulation, or distress, or persecution, or famine, or nakedness, or peril, or the sword? …For I am convinced that neither death nor life, neither angels nor demons, neither the present nor the future, nor any powers, neither height, nor depth, nor anything else in all creation, will be able to separate us from the love of God that is in Christ Jesus our Lord."* (Romans 8:35,38-39)

- *"That if you confess with your mouth, 'Jesus is Lord,' and believe in your heart that God raised Him from the dead, you will be saved. For it is with your heart that you believe and are justified, and it is with your mouth that you confess and are saved."* (Romans 10:9-10)[29]

---

[29] http://www.gotquestions.org/Book-of-Romans.html

Series III. Course I (con't)
Epistles to the Thessalonians

The first letter to the Thessalonians was likely the first of Paul's letters, probably written by the end of 52 AD, making it, so far as is now known, the oldest existent Christian document (almost all scholars hold that the gospels were written over a decade later).

The evidence of manuscripts alone is such as to set the authenticity of these letters beyond all doubt; it is in the Greek text of the Codex Sinaiticus (fourth century), Codex Vaticanus (fourth century), and Codex Alexandrinus (fifth century); it is in the Old Latin and Syriac Versions, which trace its authenticity down to the middle of the second century.

After Paul and Silas had left Philippi, during the Apostle's second missionary journey, they proceeded to Thessalonica, perhaps because there was in the city a synagogue of the Jews (Acts 17:2). Thessalonica was the capital of the Roman Province of Macedonia; it was a free city, ruled by a popular assemblyThe majority of modern scholars believe Paul wrote this letter from Corinth, although information appended to this work in many early manuscripts (e.g. Codices Alexandrinus, Mosquensis, and Angelicus) state that Paul wrote it in Athens after Timothy had returned from Macedonia, with news of the state of the church in Thessalonica (Acts 18:1-5; 1 Thess. 3:6).

The Epistles to the Thessalonians were confirming young disciples in the fundamental truths, exhorting them to continue in holiness, and comforting them. He wrote about the day of the Lord, events proceeding that day such as Apostasy and the Antichrist, and false teachers.

This book can be applied to many life situations. It gives us the confidence as Christians that dead or alive when Christ comes back we will be together with Him (1 Thessalonians 4:13-18). It assures us as Christians that we won't receive God's wrath (1 Thessalonians 5:8-9). It instructs us how to walk the Christian life daily (1 Thessalonians 4–5).

In the church of Thessalonica there were some misunderstandings about the return of Christ. Paul desired to clear them up in his letter. He also writes it as an instruction in holy living. St. Paul goes on to answer some concerns regarding the fate of those who die before the arrival of the new kingdom. Many seem to have believed that an afterlife would only be available to those who lived to see the kingdom. St. Paul explains that the dead will be resurrected, and dealt with prior to those still living, who will be taken up into the air. Thus, he assures, there is no reason to mourn the death of fellow Christians, and to do so is to show a shameful lack of faith.

The church in Thessalonica is believed to have been composed almost exclusively of Gentiles. This would reflect the ethnic and religious makeup of Thessalonica, and is supported by Paul's brief remark in 1:9 that they "turned to God from idols," a remark that would have made little sense to make to a Jewish audience. However, the Book of Acts records that there were Jews converted during Paul's initial preaching in Thessalonica, so these could well have been members of the church.

Eusebius of Caesarea, who wrote in the fourth century, states that St. Paul was beheaded in the reign of the Roman Emperor Nero. This event has been dated either to the year 64, when Rome was devastated by a fire, or a few years later, to 67.The Book of 2 Thessalonians is filled with information that explains the end times. It also exhorts us not to be idle and to work for what we have. There are also some great prayers in 2 Thessalonians that can be an example for us on how to pray for other believers today.

Summary Information:[30]

Epistles to the Thessalonians

<u>I Thessalonians</u>	
Chapters:	**5**
Verses:	**89**
<u>II Thessalonians</u>	
Chapters:	**3**
Verses:	**47**
OT Prophecies :	**0**
Verses of Prophecy (fulfilled):	**0**
Verses of Prophecy (unfulfilled):	**16**

[30] http://en.wikipedia.org/wiki/Epistles_to_the_Thessalonians

Course I (con't), *1st Epistle to the Thessalonians**
Suggested Reading Schedule and Discussion:

Week 3: Chapters 1 – 5

1. St. Paul praised the Faith of the Thessalonians. What relation did this journey have with other missionary journeys?

___

___

___

2. Describe St. Paul's vision on the Coming of the Lord and those who are asleep or still alive.

___

___

___

3. What did St. Paul mean by "sanctify you through and through"? Is it possible for one to"backslide" and what does this mean?

___

___

___

* Space is provided for additional notations at the end of the course.

Course I (con't), *2nd Epistle to the Thessalonians**
Suggested Reading Schedule and Discussion:

Week 3: Chapters 1 – 3

1. What was the purpose of 2nd Thessalonians? Was St. Paul encouraged by their loyalty and perseverance?

___

___

___

2. Why did St. Paul encourage then to stand firm? What spiritual powers were at work in his journeys?

___

___

___

3. What were his admonishments against idleness? Were there other issues which he addressed?

___

___

___

* Space is provided for additional notations at the end of the course

- *"We believe that Jesus died and rose again and so we believe that God will bring with Jesus those who have fallen asleep in him….we tell you that we who are still alive, who are left till the coming of the Lord, will certainly not precede those who have fallen asleep. For the Lord himself will come down from heaven, …with the voice of the archangel and with the trumpet call of God, and the dead in Christ will rise first. We who are still alive and are left will be caught up together with them in the clouds to meet the Lord in the air. And so we will be with the Lord forever". (1 Thessalonians 4:14-17).*

- *"Be joyful always and give thanks in all circumstances, for this is God's will for you in Christ Jesus." (1 Thessalonians 5:16).*

- *"God is just: He will pay back trouble to those who trouble you and give relief to you who are troubled, and to us as well. This will happen when the Lord Jesus is revealed from heaven in blazing fire with powerful angels. (2 Thessalonians 1:6-7).*[31]

[31] http://www.gotquestions.org/Books-of-Thessalonians.html

The End of Course One

(Please jot down any additional notations which may be helpful in group discussions.)

Series III. Course II
Epistles to the Corinthians

The epistle was written from Ephesus (16:8). According to Acts of the Apostles, Paul founded the church in Corinth (Acts 18:1-17), then spent approximately three years in Ephesus (Acts 19:8, 19:10, 20:31). The letter was written during this time in Ephesus, which is usually dated as being in the range of 53 to 57 AD.

In 16:8 Paul declares his intention of staying in Ephesus until Pentecost. This statement, in turn, is clearly reminiscent of Paul's Second Missionary Journey, when Paul travelled from Corinth to Ephesus, before going to Jerusalem for Pentecost (cf. Acts 18:22). Thus, it is possible that I Corinthians was written during Paul's first (brief) stay in Ephesus, at the end of his Second Journey, usually dated to early 54 AD.

St. Paul's claim to Apostleship begins with this passage, "Last of all, as to one untimely born, He (Jesus) appeared to me", 1 Corinthians 15:8). He later indicates that Cephas (Peter) and James also saw the risen Christ. It is no coincidence that he went purposely to visit Peter and James in Jerusalem and confirm their vision of the Lord.

The conversion of St. Paul on the road to Damascus is told three times. While St. Paul was on the road to Damascus, near Damascus, "suddenly a light from heaven flashed around him. He fell to the ground" (9:3-4), the light was "brighter than the sun" (26:13) and he was subsequently blinded for three days (9:9). He heard a voice in the Hebrew language (probably Aramaic): "Saul, Saul, why do you persecute me? ... I am Jesus" (26:14-15).

These epistles show the powerful self-control of the apostle in spite of his physical weakness, his distressed circumstances, his incessant troubles, and his emotional nature. It was written, he tells us, in bitter anguish, 'out of much affliction and pressure of heart . . . and with streaming eyes' (2 Cor 2:4); yet he restrained the expression of his feelings, and wrote with a dignity and holy calm which he thought most calculated to win back his erring children.

St. Paul writes to the Corinthians about Christian life and conduct. Noteworthy among the passages are the Gifts of the Holy Spirit (1 Corinthians 12). It contains a vigorous attack on participation in idolatry, fornication, the unveiling of women, and improper conduct at the common meal.

The second epistle was written to comfort St. Paul's rebuke and corrections in his stern first epistle to the stubborn Corinthians. Throughout the letters, Paul presents issues that are troubling the community in Corinth and offers ways to fix them. They are expected to become imitators of Jesus and follow the ways in Christ as he, Paul, teaches in all his churches (1 Cor. 4:14-16).

St. Paul perhaps strikes an early blow to rampant denominationalism in his (paraphrased) treatise, 'Do I belong to Apollos? Do I belong to Cephas (Peter)? Do I belong to St. Paul? No! Christ was crucified '.

St. Paul frequently refers to the Mosaic law, comparing it with the surpassing greatness of the gospel of Jesus Christ and salvation by grace. In 2 Corinthians 3:4-11, Paul contrasts the Old Testament law with the new covenant of grace, referring to the law as that which "kills" while the Spirit gives life. The law is the "ministry of death, written and engraved on stone"

Summary Information:[32]

Epistles to the Corinthians

<u>I Corinthians</u>	
Chapters:	**16**
Verses:	**437**
<u>II Corinthians</u>	
Chapters:	**13**
Verses:	**257**
OT Prophecies :	**9**
Verses of Prophecy (fulfilled):	**59**
Verses of Prophecy (unfulfilled):	**9**

32 http://en.wikipedia.org/wiki/Epistles_to_the_Corinthians

Course II , *1st Epistle to the Corinthians**
Suggested Reading Schedule and Discussion:

Week 4: Chapters 1 – 7

1. What does St. Paul say about boasting? Did he himself boast and what were the results?

____

____

____

2. What does he mean by "God has made foolish the wisdom of the World"? He also used the analogy of the "tree" to the Jews and the Greeks. Explain.

____

____

____

3. What was his advice on dealing with an immoral brother? Was he compassionate in this teaching?

____

____

____

* Space is provided for additional notations at the end of the course.

Course II , *1st Epistle to the Corinthians**
Suggested Reading Schedule and Discussion:

Week 5: Chapters 8 – 9, 15, 16

1. What are the rights of an Apostle? Did St. Paul force these rights upon the people to whom he ministered?

___

___

___

2. Describe St. Paul's explanation of the resurrection. How does this relate to the overall "Gospel" message?

___

___

___

3. What is St. Paul's view on anyone who does not love the Lord? Can one's view change or is it predestined?

___

___

___

* Space is provided for additional notations at the end of the course.

Course II (con't) , *2nd Epistle to the Corinthians**
Suggested Reading Schedule and Discussion:

Week 6: Chapters 8-13

1. What is the general rule and result of sowing? What is the relation of the ground in the parables?

___

___

___

2. How does St. Paul see himself as a Minister? What is his focus? Preaching? Baptism? Healing?

___

___

___

3. Discuss St. Paul's sufferings for the Gospel. Discuss St. Paul's sufferings for the Gospel of Jesus Christ.

___

___

___

* Space is provided for additional notations at the end of the course.

- *"Do you not know that your body is a temple of the Holy Spirit, who is in you, whom you have received from God? You are not your own; you were bought at a price. Therefore honor God with your body."* *(1 Corinthians 6:19-20).*

- *"For what I received I passed on to you as of first importance: that Christ died for our sins according to the Scriptures, that he was buried, that he was raised on the third day according to the Scriptures."(1 Corinthians 15:3-4).*

- *"Love is patient, love is kind. It does not envy, it does not boast, it is not proud. It is not rude, it is not self-seeking, it is not easily angered, and it keeps no record of wrongs. Love does not delight in evil but rejoices with the truth. It always protects, always trusts, always hopes, and always perseveres." (1 Corinthians 13:4-7).*

- *"Therefore, if anyone is in Christ, he is a new creation; the old has gone, the new has come!" (2 Corinthians 5:17)*[33]

[33] http://www.gotquestions.org/Books-of-Corinthians.html

The End of Course Two

(Please jot down any additional notations which may be helpful in group discussions.)

Series III. Course III
Epistles to the Ephesians & Philemon

The letter to the Ephesians is the first one of the prison epistles. The prison epistles consist of the Books of Ephesians, Philippians, Colossians and Philemon. St. Paul's first and hurried visit for the space of three months to Ephesus is recorded in Acts 18:19–21.

The work he began on this occasion was carried forward by Apollos (24–26) and Aquila and Priscilla. On his second visit early in the following year, he remained at Ephesus "three years," for he found it was the key to the western provinces of Asia Minor.

Saint Paul is traditionally said to have written the letter to the Ephesians while he was in prison in Rome (around 64 AD). This would be about the same time as the Epistle to the Colossians (which in many points it resembles) and the Epistle to Philemon It was probably written from Rome during Paul's first imprisonment (3:1; 4:1; 6:20), and probably soon after his arrival there in the year 64 AD, four years after he had parted with the Ephesian elders at Miletus.

St. Paul intended that all who long for Christ-like maturity would receive this writing. Enclosed within the Book of Ephesians is the discipline needed to develop into true children of God. Furthermore, a study in Ephesians will help to fortify and to establish the believer so he can fulfill the purpose and calling God has given.

The aim of this epistle is to confirm and to equip a maturing church. It presents a balanced view of the body of Christ and its importance in God's economy.

Ignatius of Antioch himself seemed to be very well versed in the epistle to the Ephesians, and mirrors many of his own thoughts in his own epistle to the Ephesians.

The letter to the Ephesians is the first one of the prison epistles. The prison epistles consist of the Books of Ephesians, Philippians, Colossians and Philemon.

St. Paul's first and hurried visit for the space of three months to Ephesus is recorded in Acts 18:19–21. The work he began on this occasion was carried forward by Apollos (24–26) and Aquila and Priscilla.

St. Paul's writing breaks down into three main segments. (1) Chapters one through three introduce principles with respect to God's accomplishment. (2) Chapters four and five put forth principles regarding our present existence. (3) Chapter six presents principles concerning our daily struggle.

Saint Paul is traditionally said to have written the letter to the Ephesians while he was in prison in Rome (around 64 AD). This would be about the same time as the Epistle to the Colossians (which in many points it resembles) and the Epistle to Philemon. It was probably written from Rome during Paul's first imprisonment (3:1; 4:1; 6:20), and probably soon after his arrival there in the year 64 AD, four years after he had parted with the Ephesian elders at Miletus.

St. Paul intended that all who long for Christ-like maturity would receive this writing. Enclosed within the Book of Ephesians is the discipline needed to develop into true children of God. Furthermore, a study in Ephesians will help to fortify and to establish the believer so he can fulfill the purpose and calling God has given. The aim of this epistle is to confirm and to equip a maturing church. It presents a balanced view of the body of Christ and its importance in God's economy.

Ignatius of Antioch himself seemed to be very well versed in the epistle to the Ephesians, and mirrors many of his own thoughts in his own epistle to the Ephesians Doctrine occupies the greatest portion of the Book of Ephesians. Half of the teaching in this epistle relates to our standing in Christ, and the remainder of it affects our condition. All too often those who teach from this book bypass all the foundational instruction and go directly to the closing chapter. It is this chapter that emphasizes the warfare or the struggle of the saints. However, to benefit fully from the contents of this epistle, one must begin at the beginning of Paul's instruction in this letter.

With Paul in Rome was a runaway slave named Onesimus. Onesimus had come to Paul and had become a Christian (cf. Philemon 10). Paul was obligated to return Onesimus to his rightful master, a Christian brother named Philemon. It appears that Philemon was a member of the church of Colosse. (cf. Philemon 23).

Paul wrote his letter to Philemon, in which he expressed his desire to be able to retain Onesimus' valuable services in Rome. He asked Philemon to treat Onesimus kindly as a Christian brother. Since Tychicus would be traveling to the church of Colosse, where Philemon was a member, Paul sent Onesimus back to Philemon in the company of Tychicus. Tychicus carried, in addition to Paul's letter to the Colossians, Paul's letter to Philemon.

Summary Information:[34]

Epistles to the Ephesians & Philemon	
Ephesians	
Chapters:	**6**
Verses:	**155**
Philemon	
Chapters:	**1**
Verses:	**25**
OT Prophecies :	**0**
Verses of Prophecy (fulfilled):	**1**
Verses of Prophecy (unfulfilled)	**8**

[34] http://en.wikipedia.org/wiki/Epistle_to_the_Ephesians

Course III, *Epistle to the Ephesians**
Suggested Reading Schedule and Discussion:

Week 7: Chapters 1 – 6

1. What does St. Paul keep asking God on behalf of the Ephesians ? Did he receive his prayer requests?

____

____

____

2. What are the relationships of Grace and Faith to our Salvation? To whom does God have Grace?

____

____

____

3. What is the fate of an immoral, greedy, or impure person? What are the wages of sin and what is the final disposition of such a person?

____

____

____

* Space is provided for additional notations at the end of the course

Course III (con't), *Letter to Philemon**
Suggested Reading Schedule and Discussion:

Week 7: Chapter 1

1. Why was the letter to Philemon sent and by whom? Why was the subject to controversial?

____

____

____

2. What was St.Paul's admonition on slavery? Did he justify or demonize slavery or did he answer definitively?

____

____

____

3. What relation, if any, does this story have with the Good Samaritan parable? Was Onesimus a slave by race, culture or debt servitude?

____

____

____

* Space is provided for additional notations at the end of the course.

- *"Praise be to the God and Father of our Lord Jesus Christ, who has blessed us in the heavenly realms with every spiritual blessing in Christ." (Ephesians 1:3)*

- *"For it is by grace you have been saved, through faith—and this not from yourselves, it is the gift of God—not by works, so that no one can boast...." (Ephesians 2:8-10)*

- *"There is one body and one Spirit - just as you were called to one hope when you were called - one Lord, one faith, one baptism; one God and Father of all, who is over all and through all and in all." (Ephesians 4:4-6).*

- *"Finally, be strong in the Lord and in his mighty power. Put on the full armor of God so that you can take your stand against the devil's schemes." (Ephesians 6:10-11)*

- *"...no longer as a slave, but better than a slave, as a dear brother. He is very dear to me but even dearer to you, both as a man and as a brother in the Lord." (Philemon 1:16)*[35]

[35] http://www.gotquestions.org/Book-of-Ephesians.html

Series III. Course III (con't)

Epistle to the Philippians

Philippians 1:1 identifies the author of the Book of Philippians as the apostle Paul, likely along with the help of Timothy. Philippi is the first place in Europe where the gospel was preached. This church, along with the other churches of Macedonia, had made a name for themselves when it came to liberality (II Corinthians 8:1-5). St. Paul refers to them as "my beloved and longed-for brethren, my joy and crown" (Philippians 4:1).

The Epistle to the Philippians, one of Paul's prison epistles, was written in Rome. It was at Philippi, which the apostle visited on his second missionary journey (Acts 16:12), that Lydia and the Philippian jailer and his family were converted to Christ. Now, some few years later, the church was well established, as may be inferred from its address which includes "bishops (elders) and deacons" (Philippians 1:1).The occasion of the epistle was to acknowledge a gift of money from the church at Philippi, brought to the apostle by Epaphroditus, one of its members (Philippians 4:10-18).

This is a tender letter to a group of Christians who were especially close to the heart of Paul (2 Corinthians 8:1-6), and comparatively little is said about doctrinal error. Philippians can be called "Resources Through Suffering." The book is about Christ in our life, Christ in our mind, Christ as our goal, Christ as our strength, and joy through suffering. It was written during Paul's imprisonment in Rome, about thirty years after Christ's ascension and about ten years after Paul first preached at Philippi.

Philippians is perhaps St. Paul's "happiest" letter. And the happiness is infectious. Before we've read a dozen lines, we begin to feel the joy ourselves—the dance of words and the exclamations of delight have a way of getting inside us.

St. Paul was Nero's prisoner, yet the epistle fairly shouts with triumph, the words "joy" and "rejoice" appearing frequently (Philippians 1:4, 18, 25, 26; 2:2, 28; Philippians 3:1, 4:1, 4, 10).

Right Christian experience is the outworking, whatever our circumstances may be, of the life, nature, and mind of Christ living in us (Philippians 1:6, 11; 2:5, 13). Philippians reaches its pinnacle at 2:5-11 with the glorious and profound declaration regarding the humiliation and exaltation of our Lord Jesus Christ. Philippians may be divided as follows:

1. Introduction, 1:1-7
2. Christ the Christian's Life: Rejoicing in Spite of Suffering, 1:8-30
3. Christ the Christian's Pattern: Rejoicing in Lowly Service, 2:1-30
4. Christ the Object of the Christian's Faith, Desire, and Expectation, 3:1-21
5. Christ the Christian's Strength: Rejoicing Through Anxiety, 4:1-9
6. Conclusion, 4:10-23

When we read what Paul wrote to the believers in the city of Philippi, we find ourselves in the company of just such a master. Paul doesn't tell us that we can be happy, or how to be happy. He simply and unmistakably is happy. None of his circumstances contribute to his joy. He wrote from a jail cell, his work was under attack by competitors, and after twenty years Philemon.

Summary Information:[36]

Epistle to the Philippians	
Chapters:	**4**
Verses:	**104**
OT Prophecies :	**0**
Verses of Prophecy (fulfilled):	**0**
Verses of Prophecy (unfulfilled):	**5**

[36] http://en.wikipedia.org/wiki/Epistle_to_the_Philippians

Course III (con't) , *Epistle to the Philippians**
Suggested Reading Schedule and Discussion:

Week 8: Chapters 1 – 3

1. What does St. Paul mean when he refers to "his chains"? Did he ever wish to free himself of his chains?

___

___

___

2. What does St. Paul mean when he is "pressing on toward the goal"? What analogy to this passage would St. Paul have gotten from the Roman coliseums?

___

___

___

3. How does one imitate Christ's humility according St. Paul? Did St. Paul exhibit such humility and when did he boast?

___

___

___

* Space is provided for additional notations at the end of the course.

- *And this is my prayer: that your love may abound more and more in knowledge and depth of insight, so that you may be able to discern what is best and may be pure and blameless for the day of Christ, filled with the fruit of righteousness that comes through Jesus Christ—to the glory and praise of God. (Philippians 1:9-11)*

- *"For to me, to live is Christ, and to die is gain." (Philippians 1:21)*

- *"But whatever was to my profit I now consider loss for the sake of Christ." (Philippians 3:7)*

- *"Rejoice in the Lord always. I will say it again: Rejoice!" (Philippians 4:4)*

- *"Do not be anxious about anything, but in everything, by prayer and petition, with thanksgiving, present your requests to God. And the peace of God, which transcends all understanding, will guard your hearts and your minds in Christ Jesus."(Philippians 4:6-7).*[37]

[37] http://www.gotquestions.org/Book-of-Philippians.html

Series III. Course III (con't)
Epistle to the Colossians

The apostle Paul was the primary writer of the Book of Colossians (Colossians 1:13). Timothy is also given some credit (Colossians 1:1). It was written, (according to the text), by Paul the Apostle to the Church in Colossae, a small Phrygian city near Laodicea and approximately 100 miles from Ephesus in Asia Minor.

The Book of Colossians is a mini-ethics course, addressing every area of Christian life. Paul progresses from the individual life to the home and family, from work to the way we should treat others. The theme of this book is the sufficiency of our Lord, Jesus Christ, in meeting our needs in every area. Colossians was written explicitly to defeat the heresy that had arisen in Colosse, which endangered the existence of the church.

While we do not know what was told to Paul, this letter is his response We can surmise based on Paul's response that he was dealing with a defective view of Christ (denying His real and true humanity and not accepting His full deity). Paul appears also to dispute the "Jewish" emphasis on circumcision and traditions (Colossians 2:8-11; 3:11). The heresy addressed appears to be either a Jewish-Gnosticism or a mix between Jewish asceticism and Greek (Stoic?) philosophy. He does a remarkable job in pointing us to the sufficiency of Christ.

The Book of Colossians contains doctrinal instruction about the deity of Christ and false philosophies (1:15-2:23), as well as practical exhortations regarding Christian conduct, including friends and speech (3:1-4:18).

The doctrinal part comprises the first two chapters. Its main theme is developed in chapter 2, with a warning against being drawn away from

Him in whom dwelt all the fullness of the deity, and who was the head of all spiritual powers. Christ was the head of the body of which they were members; and if they were truly united to him, what more did they need?

Colosse is in the region of the seven churches of Revelation 1-3. In Colossians 4:13 there is mention of local brethren in Colosse, Laodicea, and Hierapolis. Colosse was approximately 12 miles from Laodicea and 14 miles from Hierapolis Members of the congregation at Colosse had incorporated pagan elements into their practice, including worship of elemental spirits.

The Epistle to the Colossians declares Christ's supremacy over the entire created universe and exhorts Christians to lead godly lives. The letter consists of two parts: first a doctrinal section, then a second regarding conduct. In both sections, false teachers who have been spreading error in the congregation are opposed.

Paul countered this error in Colossians 2:11-15 in which he declares that circumcision of the flesh was no longer necessary because Christ had come. His was a circumcision of the heart, not the flesh, making the ceremonial rites of the Old Testament law no longer necessary (Deuteronomy 10:16, 30:6; Jeremiah 4:4, 9:26; Acts 7:51; Romans 2:29).

Tychicus is named as the bearer of the letter, just as he is in Ephesians and Philemon, and he is to tell the recipients of the state of the apostle. After friendly greetings, he bids them exchange this letter with the one he had sent to the neighboring Laodicea Church. (The apocryphal Epistle to the Laodiceans was almost certainly forged based on this instruction.) He then closes the letter with the usual salutation.

The issue of Jewish legalism in Colosse was of great concern to Paul. So radical was the concept of salvation by grace apart from works that those steeped in Old Testament law found it very difficult to grasp. Consequently, there was a continual movement among the legalists to add certain requirements from the law to this new faith. Primary among them was the requirement of circumcision which was still practiced among some of the Jewish converts.

Summary Information:[38]

Epistle to the Colossians	
Chapters:	**4**
Verses:	**95**
OT Prophecies :	**0**
Verses of Prophecy (fulfilled):	**0**
Verses of Prophecy (unfulfilled):	**3**

[38] http://en.wikipedia.org/wiki/Epistle_to_the_Colossians

Course III (con't) , *Epistle to the Colossians**
Suggested Reading Schedule and Discussion:

Week 8: Chapters 1 – 4

1. What is Christ's relation to God and the Church? When was the Trinity conceived and by whom?

___

___

___

2. What are St.Paul' s thoughts on deceptive philosophy and human tradition? Did he encounter such philosophies? When and where?

___

___

___

3. What are the rules for holy living? What is the response when and if one breaks these rules?

___

___

___

* Space is provided for additional notations at the end of the course.

- *The Son is the image of the invisible God, the firstborn over all creation. For in him all things were created: things in heaven and on earth, visible and invisible, whether thrones or powers or rulers or authorities; all things have been created through him and for him. He is before all things, and in him all things hold together. And he is the head of the body, the church; he is the beginning and the firstborn from among the dead, so that in everything he might have the supremacy" (Colossians 1:15-18)*

- *"See to it that no one takes you captive through hollow and deceptive philosophy, which depends on human tradition...of this world rather than on Christ." (Colossians 2:8).*

- *"Therefore, as God's chosen people, holy and dearly loved, clothe yourselves with compassion, kindness, humility, gentleness and patience. Bear with each other and forgive whatever grievances you may have against one another. Forgive as the Lord forgave you." (Colossians 3:12-13)*[39]

---

[39] http://www.gotquestions.org/Book-of-Colissians.html

Series III. Course III (con't)
Epistle to the Galatians

Galatians 1:1 clearly identifies the Apostle Paul as the writer of the Epistle to the Galatians. It is a letter from Paul of Tarsus to a number of Early Christian communities in the Roman province of Galatia in central Anatolia.

No original of the letter is known to survive. The earliest reasonably complete version available to scholars today, named P46, dates to approximately the year 200 A.D., approximately 150 years after the original was presumably drafted.

Paul's letter is addressed "to the churches in Galatia" (Galatians 1:2), but the location of these churches is a matter of debate. A minority of scholars have argued that the "Galatia" is an ethnic reference to a Celtic people living in northern Asia Minor, but most agree that it is a geographical reference to the Roman province in central Asia Minor, which had been settled by immigrant Celts in the 270s BC and retained Gaulish features of culture and language in Paul's day Acts of the Apostles records Paul traveling to the "region of Galatia and Phrygia", which lay immediately west of Galatia. The main theme was that the people of Galatia have turned away from Paul's teachings.

The churches in Galatia were formed partly of converted Jews and partly of Gentile converts, as was generally the case. Paul asserts his apostolic character and the doctrines he taught, that he might confirm the Galatian churches in the faith of Christ, especially with respect to the important point of justification by faith alone. Thus the subject is mainly the same as that which is discussed in the Epistle to the Romans, that is, justification by faith alone.

In this epistle, however, attention is particularly directed to the point that men are justified by faith without the works of the Law of Moses. The essential truth of justification by faith rather than by the works of the law had been obscured by the Judaizers' insistence that believers in Christ must keep the law if they expected to be perfect before God.

When Paul learned that this teaching had begun to penetrate the Galatian churches and that it had alienated them from their heritage of liberty, he wrote the impassioned remonstrance contained in this epistle.

The Book of Galatians was originally written as a letter to the Christians in southern Galatia where on his first missionary journey St. Paul established the congregations in Pisidia Antioch, Iconium, Lystra, and Derbe. Galatians was written as a protest against corruption of the gospel of Christ. The essential truth of justification by faith rather than by the works of the law had been obscured.

One of the main themes of the Book of Galatians is found in 3:11: "The righteous shall live by faith." Not only are we saved by faith (John 3:16; Ephesians 2:8-9), but the life of the believer in Christ—day by day, moment by moment—is lived by and through that faith.

Throughout Paul's Epistle to the Galatians, saving grace—the gift of God—is juxtaposed against the law of Moses, which does not save. The themes connecting Galatians to the Old Testament center around the law vs. grace: the inability of the law to justify (2:16); the believer's deadness to the law (2:19); Abraham's justification by faith (3:6); the law bringing not salvation but God's wrath (3:10); and love, not works, fulfilling the law (5:14).

The result of justification by grace through faith is spiritual freedom. Paul appealed to the Galatians to stand fast in their freedom, and not get "entangled again with a yoke of bondage (that is, the Mosaic law)" (Galatians 5:1).

Christian freedom is not an excuse to gratify one's lower nature; rather, it is an opportunity to love one another (Galatians 5:13; 6:7-10). Such freedom does not insulate one from life's struggles. Indeed, it may intensify the battle between the Spirit and the flesh. Nevertheless, the flesh (the lower nature) has been crucified with Christ (Galatians 2:20); and, as a consequence, the Spirit will bear His fruit such as love, joy, and peace in the life of the believer (Galatians 5:22-23).

Summary Information:[40]

Epistle to the Galatians	
Chapters:	**6**
Verses:	**149**
OT Prophecies :	**0**
Verses of Prophecy (fulfilled):	**1**
Verses of Prophecy (unfulfilled):	**4**

[40] http://en.wikipedia.org/wiki/Epistle_to_the_Galatians

Course III (con't) , *Epistle to the Galatians**
Suggested Reading Schedule and Discussion:

Week 9: Chapters 1 – 6

1. What was St. Paul's background in Judaism? Did this help or hinder his ministry for Christ?

___

___

___

2. What did St. Paul do to be accepted by the Apostles? Was he accepted and by whom?

___

___

___

3. What was the reasons for St. Paul's opposition to St. Peter? Did the great Apostles reconcile and under what conditions?

___

___

___

* Space is provided for additional notations at the end of the course.

- *Knowing that a man is not justified by the works of the law, but by the faith of Jesus Christ, even we have believed in Jesus Christ, that we might be justified by the faith of Christ, and not by the works of the law: for by the works of the law shall no flesh be justified." (Galatians 2:16).*

- *"I have been crucified with Christ and I no longer live, but Christ lives in me. The life I live in the body, I live by faith in the Son of God, who loved me and gave himself for me." (Galatians 2:20)*

- *"to redeem those under law, that we might receive the full rights of sons. Because you are sons, God sent the Spirit of his Son into our hearts, the Spirit who calls out, 'Abba, Father.'" (Galatians 4:5-6)*

- *"But the fruit of the Spirit is love, joy, peace, patience, kindness, goodness, faithfulness, gentleness and self-control. Against such things there is no law." (Galatians 5:22-23)*[41]

---

41 http://www.gotquestions.org/Book-of-Galatians.html

Series III. Course III (con't)
Epistles to Timothy & Titus

The First Epistle to Timothy is one of three letters in New Testament of the Bible often grouped together as the Pastoral Epistles. (The others are Second Timothy and Titus.) The letter, traditionally attributed to Saint Paul, consists mainly of counsels to his colleague and delegate Timothy regarding his ministry in Ephesus.

The genuineness of Pauline authorship was accepted by Church orthodoxy as early as c. 180 AD, as evidenced by the surviving testimony of Irenaeus and the author of the Muratorian fragment. Possible allusions are found in the letters from Clement of Rome to the Corinthians (c. 95 AD), Ignatius of Antioch to the Ephesians (c. 110 AD) and Polycarp to the Philippians (c. 130 AD).

St. Paul wrote to Timothy to encourage him in his responsibility for overseeing the work of the Ephesian church and possibly the other churches in the province of Asia (1 Timothy 1:3).

This letter lays the foundation for ordaining elders (1 Timothy 3:1-7), and provides guidance for ordaining people into offices of the church.The historical relationship between Paul and Timothy is one of mentorship. Timothy is first mentioned in Acts 16:1. His mother Eunice, and his grandmother, Lois, are mentioned in 2 Tim. 1:5. All that we know of his father is that he was a Greek not a Jew (Acts 16:1).

Timothy's official position in the church was one of an evangelist (1 Timothy 4:14) and he worked with Paul in Phrygia, Galatia, and Mysia, Troa, Philippi and Berea (Acts 17:14) and continued on to do even more work in Athens, and Thessalonica for the church (Acts 17:15;

1 Thessalonians 3:2) not to mention his work in Corinth, Macedonia, Ephesus and greater Asia. Timothy was also noted for coming to Paul's aid when Paul fell into prison (Philippians 1:1, 2 Timothy 4:13).

The Epistle to Titus is known as one of the Pastoral Epistles as are the two letters to Timothy. This epistle was written by the apostle Paul to encourage his brother in the faith, Titus, whom he had left in Crete to lead the church which Paul had established on one of his missionary journeys (Titus 1:5).

The first letter of St. Paul to Timothy instructed a young pastor who had been a help of St. Paul in his work. Timothy was a Greek. His mother was a Jewess and his father was Greek. St. Paul was more than just a mentor and leader to Timothy, he was like a father to him and Timothy was like a son to St. Paul (1 Timothy 1:2). St. Paul begins the letter by urging Timothy to be on the guard for false teachers and false doctrine. Much of the letter deals with pastoral conduct...St. Paul encourages Timothy to stand firm...and to remain true to his calling.

After his release Paul sailed from Rome into Asia, passing Crete by the way, and there he left Titus "to set in order the things that were wanting." Thence he would have gone to Ephesus, where he left Timothy, and from Ephesus to Macedonia, where he wrote the *First Epistle to Timothy*, and thence, according to the superscription of this epistle, to Nicopolis in Epirus, from which place he wrote to Titus, about 66 or 67 AD.

St. Paul encourages Timothy to remain passionate for Christ and to remain firm in sound doctrine (2 Timothy 1:1-2, 13-14). Paul reminds Timothy to avoid ungodly beliefs and practices and to flee from anything immoral (2 Timothy 2:14-26). In the end times there will be both intense persecution and apostasy from the Christian faith (2 Timothy 3:1-17). St. Paul closes with an intense plea for believers to stand firm in the faith and to finish the race strong (2 Timothy 4:1-8).

The Book of 2 Timothy is essentially St. Paul's "last words." He wanted to encourage Timothy, and all other believers, to persevere in faith (2 Timothy 3:14) and proclaim the Gospel of Jesus Christ (2 Timothy 4:2). In his Second Letter to Timothy shortly before his martyrdom St. Paul asked Timothy to come to him in Rome, for he longed to see Timothy yet once more (cf. 2 Timothy 1:4; 4:9,21).

Summary Information:[42][43]

Epistles to Timothy & Titus

I Timothy	
Chapters:	**6**
Verses:	**113**
II Timothy	
Chapters:	**4**
Verses:	**83**
Titus	
Chapters:	**3**
Verses:	**46**
OT Prophecies :	**0**
Verses of Prophecy (fulfilled):	**15**
Verses of Prophecy (unfulfilled) :	**8**

[42] http://en.wikipedia.org/wiki/Epistles_to_Timothy
[43] http://en.wikipedia.org/wiki/Epistle_to_Titus

Course III (con't) , *1st Epistle to Timothy**
Suggested Reading Schedule and Discussion:

Week 10: Chapters 1 –4

1. Did St. Paul consider himself a sinner? What was his remedy for his fallen state and was that permanent?

2. Who was St. Timothy and what was his relation to St. Paul? On what missionary journeys did St. Timothy accompany St. Paul?

3. What was St. Paul's position on worship in church and women's interaction? How do we reconcile that with today's church and the expanding role of women?

* Space is provided for additional notations at the end of the course.

Course III (con't) , *2nd Epistle to Timothy**
Suggested Reading Schedule and Discussion:

Week 10: Chapters 1 –3

1. What was St. Paul's position on quarreling? Are there good reasons to quarrel among the brethren?

____

____

____

2. What was St. Paul's charge to St. Timothy? Was St. Timothy true to that charge and calling?

____

____

____

3. Describe St. Paul's differences from the other Apostles. Why was he the appropriate one to write most of the epistles in the New Testament?

____

____

____

* Space is provided for additional notations at the end of the course.

- *"For God did not give us a spirit of timidity, but a spirit of power, of love and of self-discipline." (2 Timothy 1:7).*

- *"Preach the Word; be prepared in season and out of season; correct, rebuke and encourage—with great patience and careful instruction." (2 Timothy 4:2).*

- *Fight the good fight of the faith. Take hold of the eternal life to which you were called when you made your good confession in the presence of many witnesses." (1 Timothy 6:12).*

- *"At one time we too were foolish, disobedient, deceived and enslaved by passions and pleasures... But when the kindness and love of God our Savior appeared, he saved us... He saved us through...renewal by the Holy Spirit, whom he poured out on us ...through Jesus Christ our Savior." (Titus 3:3-6).*[44]

[44] http://www.gotquestions.org/Books-of-Timothy.html

The End of Course Three

(Please jot down any additional notations which may be helpful in group discussions.)

IV. MAJOR APOSTLES SERIES

The Letters of St. James, St. Peter and St. John, the Hebrew epistle of St. Paul and Revelation of St. John.

St. Paul was later called by the Resurrected Lord as an Apostle on the Damascus road The 'inner circle' of Christ's initial 12 Apostles were Saints James, John and Peter. These three were with Jesus throughout his 3-year ministry on earth and were eye-witnesses and writers of His many miracles, healings and resurrection appearances. The book of Revelation is the culmination of the Old Testament Verses of Prophecy in Daniel, Isaiah, Ezekiel and Zechariah about the end times.

Course One:	**Epistle to the Hebrews**
Course Two:	**The Letter of St. James** **The Letters of St. Peter** **The Letters of St. John**
Course Three:	**The Revelation of St. John**

Series IV. Course I
Epistle to the Hebrews

The Book of Hebrews addresses three separate groups: believers in Christ, unbelievers who had knowledge of and an intellectual acceptance of the facts of Christ, and unbelievers who were attracted to Christ, but who rejected Him ultimately.

"The book of Hebrews was written by a Hebrew to other Hebrews telling the Hebrews to stop acting like Hebrews". In other words, many of the early Jewish believers were slipping back into the rites and rituals of Judaism in order to escape the mounting persecution. This letter, then, is an exhortation for those persecuted believers to continue in the grace of Jesus Christ.

The writer of Hebrews continually makes mention of the superiority of Christ in both His personage and in His ministering work. Hebrews tells us that Christ Jesus is better than anything mere religion has to offer. All the pomp and circumstance of religion pales in comparison to the person, work, and ministry of Christ Jesus. It is the superiority of our Lord Jesus, then, that remains the theme of this eloquently written letter.

The writer of Hebrews gives ample encouragement to believers, but there are five solemn warnings we must heed. There is the danger of neglect (Hebrews 2:1-4), the danger of unbelief (Hebrews 3:7–4:13), the danger of spiritual immaturity (Hebrews 5:11–6:20), the danger of failing to endure (Hebrews 10:26-39), and the inherent danger of refusing God (Hebrews 12:25-29).).

The fact that Timothy was alive at the time the epistle was written and the absence of any evidence showing the end of the Old Testament sacrificial system that occurred with Jerusalem's destruction in 70 AD, indicates the book was written around 65 AD.

Most scholars today believe the document was written to prevent apostasy. The Epistle emphasizes non-Jewish followers of Jesus do not need to convert to Judaism to share in God's promises to Jews.

Hebrews tells us that Christ Jesus is better than anything mere religion has to offer. All the pomp and circumstance of religion pales in comparison to the person, work, and ministry of Christ Jesus. It is the superiority of our Lord Jesus, then, that remains the theme of this eloquently written letter.

The Epistle to the Hebrews was thought by some in antiquity such as Clement of Alexandria to be the fourteenth letter of Paul. The early church largely agreed. Jerome and Augustine of Hippo were influential in affirming Paul's authorship. Eusebius reports that the original letter was written in Hebrew and, later, Greek.

On the other hand, there has been some discussion through the centuries that Paul was not the writer due to the writing style of the book of Hebrews and that his salutation was missing. Origen of Alexandria (c. 240 AD) suggested that either Luke the Evangelist or Clement of Rome might be the author. Tertullian proposed Paul's companion Barnabas. The conclusion might well be that, although Paul may have not actually written sections of the Epistle, he was very influential and had close contact and input with the writer(s).

The early church father Clement quoted from the Book of Hebrews in A.D. 95. However, internal evidence such as the fact that Timothy was alive at the time the epistle was written and the absence of any evidence showing the end of the Old Testament sacrificial system that occurred with Jerusalem's destruction in A.D. 70 indicates the book was written around A.D. 65.

Although some include the Book of Hebrews among the apostle Paul's writings, the certain identity of the author remains an enigma. Missing is Paul's customary salutation common to his other works.[45]

Summary Information:[46]

Book of Hebrews	
Chapters:	**13**
Verses:	**303**
OT Prophecies:	**0**
Verses of Prophecy (fulfilled):	**9**
Verses of Prophecy (unfulfilled):	**24**

Additional References and Peripheral Study Guides

- *Donald Guthrie, New Testament Introduction, (Illinois, Inter-Varsity Press, 1976)*
- *George Ladd, A Theology of the New Testament, (Grand Rapids, Eerdmans's ,1974)*
- *Justo Gonzalez, A History of Christian Thought, vol 1, (Nashville, Abingdon , 1970)*
- *Bruce Chilton, Rabbi Paul, (New York, DoubleDay Publishers, 2005)*

---

45 http://www.gotquestions.org/Book-of-Hebrews.html
46 http://en.wikipedia.org/wiki/Epistle_to_the_Hebrews

Course I, *Book of Hebrews**
Suggested Reading Schedule and Discussion:

Week 1: Chapters 1 – 7

1. Who is the Apostle and High Priest whom we confess? Why is this a direct relation of Christianity to Judaism?

___

___

___

2. Who was Melchizedek, the priest, and why is Jesus Christ likened to him? What was his relation to Abram?

___

___

___

3. Is it impossible for those who have been truly enlightened to “fall back”? Is this scriptural?

___

___

___

* Space is provided for additional notations at the end of the course.

Course I, *Book of Hebrews**
Suggested Reading Schedule and Discussion:

Week 2: Chapters 8 –13

1. What is the "New Covenant"? Is this covenant for all peoples on the earth? Are there any conditions?

___

___

___

2. Describe worship in the early Tabernacle and how that differed from worship after Christ's appearance and ministry? Describe the concept of the "sacrificial lamb".

___

___

___

3. What does the Hebrew writer say about Faith? When and how do we perceive faith in the natural order?

___

___

___

* Space is provided for additional notations at the end of the course.

- *"In the past God spoke to our forefathers through the prophets at many times and in various ways, but in these last days he has spoken to us by his Son, whom he appointed heir of all things, and through whom he made the universe." (Hebrews 1:1-2).*

- *"Therefore, since we have a great high priest who has gone through the heavens, Jesus the Son of God, let us hold firmly to the faith we profess. ...Let us then approach the throne of grace with confidence, so that we may receive mercy and find grace to help us in our time of need (Hebrews 4:14-16).*

- *"Now faith is being sure of what we hope for and certain of what we do not see." (Hebrews 11:1).*

- *"Therefore, since we are surrounded by such a great cloud of witnesses, ... Let us fix our eyes on Jesus, the author and perfecter of our faith, who for the joy set before him endured the cross, scorning its shame, and sat down at the right hand of the throne of God." " (Hebrews 12:1-2).*[47]

[47] http://www.gotquestions.org/Book-of-Hebrews.html

The End of Course One

(Please jot down any additional notations which may be helpful in group discussions.)

Series IV. Course II
Letter of St. James

The author identifies himself as "James, a servant of God and of the Lord Jesus Christ". He is traditionally understood as James the Just, the half-brother of Jesus and first bishop of Jerusalem. He is oftentimes misunderstood as James, the son of Zebedee, brother of John and one of Jesus' twelve Apostles. The epistle was addressed to "the twelve tribes scattered abroad" (James 1:1).

The book of James is probably the oldest book of the New Testament, written perhaps as early as 45 AD, before the first council of Jerusalem in 50 AD. James was martyred in approximately 62 AD, according to the historian Josephus.

Martin Luther, who detested this letter and called it "the epistle of straw," failed to recognize that James's teaching on works complemented—not contradicted—Paul's teaching on faith. While Pauline teachings concentrate on our justification with God, James' teachings concentrate on the works that exemplify that justification. James was writing to Jews to encourage them to continue growing in this new Christian faith,

James gives a particularly severe rebuke to the rich who hoard and those who are self-reliant. Finally, he ends with encouragement to believers to be patient in suffering, praying and caring for one another and bolstering our faith through fellowship.

James begins in the first chapter by describing the overall traits of the faith walk. In chapter two and the beginning of chapter three he discusses social justice and a discourse on faith in action. He then compares and contrasts the difference between worldly and godly wisdom and asks us to turn away from evil and draw close to God.

The epistle also puts to rest the idea that one can become a Christian and yet continue living in sin, exhibiting no fruit of righteousness. Such a "faith," James declares, is shared by the demons who "believe and tremble".

As indicated, a few scholars maintain that it was authored by St. James, son of Zebedee was one of the Twelve Apostles of Jesus. He was a son of Zebedee and Salome, and brother of John the Apostle. He is also called James the Greater to distinguish him from James, son of Alphaeus, who is also known as James the Less. James is described as one of the first disciples to join Jesus.

The Epistle was definitely quoted by Origen of Alexandria, and possibly a bit earlier by Irenaeus of Lyons as well as Clement of Alexandria in a lost work according to Eusebius. The Epistle of James was included among the 27 New Testament books first listed by Athanasius of Alexandria and was confirmed as a canonical epistle of the New Testament by a series of councils in the fourth century.

The book of James outlines the faith walk through genuine religion (1:1-27), genuine faith (2:1-3:12) and genuine wisdom (3:13-5:20). This book contains a remarkable parallel to Jesus' Sermon on the Mount in Matthew 5-7.

The Epistle of James is one of the most important works of the New Testament, for the important concept of faith without works is dead is expressed in this Letter in Chapter Two.

We see in the Book of James a challenge to faithful followers of Jesus Christ to not just "talk the talk," but to "walk the walk." While our faith walk, to be certain, requires a growth of knowledge about the Word, James exhorts us to not stop there. Many Christians will find this epistle challenging as James presents 60 obligations in only 108 verses. He focuses on the truths of Jesus' words in the Sermon on the Mount and motivates us to act upon what He taught.

Summary Information:[48]

Letter of James	
Chapters:	**5**
Verses:	**108**
OT Prophecies:	**0**
Verses of Prophecy (fulfilled):	**8**
Verses of Prophecy (unfulfilled):	**0**

48 http://en.wikipedia.org/wiki/Epistle_of_James

Course II, *Letter of St. James**
Suggested Reading Schedule and Discussion:

Week 3: Chapters 1 –5

1. Who was St. James, the writer of the Letter? There were two other St. James of some importance. Can you name them?

___

___

___

2. What does St. James emphasize that is necessary in addition to Faith? *Martin Luther called this book the epistle of straw because of this emphasis.*

___

___

___

3. Why does the writer of Hebrews say that we do not get what we ask? What is the model for prayer?

___

___

___

* Space is provided for additional notations at the end of the course.

- *Consider it pure joy, my brothers, whenever you face trials of many kinds, because you know that the testing of your faith develops perseverance." (James 1:2-3).*

- *"In the same way, faith by itself, if it is not accompanied by action, is dead. But someone will say, 'You have faith; I have deeds.' Show me your faith without deeds, and I will show you my faith by what I do." (James 2:17-18).*

- *"Likewise the tongue is a small part of the body, but it makes great boasts. Consider what a great forest is set on fire by a small spark." (James 3:5).*

- *Who is wise and understanding among you? Let him show it by his good life, by deeds done in the humility that comes from wisdom. 14But if you harbor bitter envy and selfish ambition in your hearts, do not boast about it or deny the truth. 15Such "wisdom" does not come down from heaven but is earthly, unspiritual, of the devil. 16For where you have envy and selfish ambition, there you find disorder and every evil practice. (James 3:13-16).*[49]

---

[49] http://www.gotquestions.org/Book-of-James.html

Series IV. Course II (con't)
Letters of St. Peter

Saint Peter (Greek: **Πέτρος, *Pétros*** "Rock", *Kephas* in Hellenized Aramaic) (c.1–68 AD) was a leader of the early Christian church. Peter was to become the first apostle ordained by Jesus in the early church.

1 Peter 1:1 identifies the author of the book of 1 Peter as the Apostle Peter. The book of 2 Peter was written toward the end of Peter's life. Since Peter was martyred in Rome during the reign of Nero, his death must have occurred prior to 68 AD. He very likely wrote 2 Peter between 65 and 68 AD.

Paul affirms that Peter had the special charge of being Apostle to the Jews, just as he, Paul, was Apostle to the Gentiles. The Gospel of Matthew recorded that Jesus told Peter: "You are *Peter*, and on this *rock* I will build my Church." Roman Catholic tradition states that he was the first Pope, the Bishop of Rome (from 30 AD to 64 AD), the author of two canonical epistles, and a martyr under Nero, crucified head down, and buried in Rome in 64 – 67 AD.

St. Peter was alarmed that false teachers were beginning to infiltrate the churches. He called on Christians to grow and become strong in their faith so that they could detect and combat the spreading apostasy. He strongly stressed the authenticity of the Word of God and the return of the Lord Jesus.

In John's gospel, Peter is the first person to enter the empty tomb, although the women and the beloved disciple see it before him (John 20:1–9). In Luke's account, the women's report of the empty tomb is dismissed by the apostles.

Peter is the one who checks for himself. The Apostle Peter wrote the first epistle to the Christians of Asia to confirm them in the Faith, to console them amid their tribulations, and to indicate to them the line of conduct to follow in suffering. Peter wrote the second epistle to excite Christians to the practice of virtue and chiefly to turn them away from false teachers.

1 Peter is a letter from Peter to the believers who had been dispersed throughout the ancient world and were under intense persecution. If anyone understood persecution, it was Peter. He was beaten, threatened, punished and jailed for preaching the Word of God. He knew what it took to endure without bitterness, without losing hope and in great faith living an obedient, victorious life.

This letter makes reference to Peter's personal experiences with Jesus and his sermons from the book of Acts. Peter confirms Satan as the great enemy of every Christian but the assurance of Christ's future return gives the incentive of hope.

Knowing that his time was short (2 Peter 1:13-15) and these churches faced immediate danger (2 Peter 2:1-3), Peter called upon the readers to refresh their memories (2 Peter 1:13) and stimulate their thinking (2 Peter 3:1-2) so that they would remember his teaching (2 Peter 1:15).

He challenged the believers to become more mature in their faith by adding to its specific Christians virtues, thereby becoming effective and productive in their knowledge of Jesus Christ (2 Peter 1:5-9). The Old and New Testament writers were set forth as their authority for their faith (2 Peter 1:12-21, 3:2, 3:15-16). Peter desired they become strong in their faith to withstand the false teachers that had crept in and adversely affected the churches.

For the Christians, Peter taught that the Second Coming is the incentive for holy living (2 Peter 3:14). After a final warning, Peter again encouraged them to grow in the grace and knowledge of their Lord and Savior Jesus Christ. He concluded with a word of praise to his Lord and Savior (2 Peter 3:18).

Summary Information:[50]

Letters of Peter

I Peter	
Chapters:	**5**
Verses:	**105**
II Peter	
Chapters:	**3**
Verses:	**61**
OT Prophecies :	**0**
Verses of Prophecy (fulfilled):	**5**
Verses of Prophecy (unfulfilled):	**18**

[50] ttp://en.wikipedia.org/wiki/Epistles_of_Peter

Course II (con't), *1st Letter of St. Peter**
Suggested Reading Schedule and Discussion:

Week 4: Chapters 1 – 5

1. To what should we set our minds and hopes? Why is this focus so Important in our daily lives?

___

___

___

2. What is the word that was preached? Who is referred to as the "incarnate word"?

___

___

___

3. What are the instructions to husbands and wives? Are these admonishments true in our modern world?

___

___

___

* Space is provided for additional notations at the end of the course.

Course II (con't), *2nd Letter of St. Peter**
Suggested Reading Schedule and Discussion:

Week 4: Chapters 1 - 3

1. What did St. Peter hear when he was on the sacred mountain? What was the context of this experience?

____

____

____

2. What does St. Peter say about the "Day of the Lord"? What relation does that have to the present time?

____

____

____

3. What does St. Peter say about false prophets and false teachers? Do we encounter falseness today in religion? How do we know the true spiritual path?

____

____

____

* Space is provided for additional notations at the end of the course.

- *For you know that it was not with perishable things such as silver or gold that you were redeemed from the empty way of life handed down to you from your forefathers, but with the precious blood of Christ, a lamb without blemish or defect. (I Peter 1:18,19).*

- *He himself bore our sins in his body on the tree, so that we might die to sins and live for righteousness; by his wounds you have been healed. (I Peter 2:24).*

- *Be self-controlled and alert. Your enemy the devil prowls around like a roaring lion looking for someone to devour. (I Peter 5:8).*

- *"His divine power has given us everything we need for life and godliness through our knowledge of Him who called us by His own glory and goodness. Through these He has given us His very great and precious promises, so that through them you may participate in the divine nature and escape the corruption in the world caused by evil desires." (2 Peter 1:3-4).*[51]

[51] http://www.gotquestions.org/Books-of-Peter.html

Series IV. Course II (con't)
Letters of St. John

Some scholars suggest that its sacred writer was not John the Apostle but John the Presbyter; however, the majority of scholars and the Catholic position have traced the Apostolic origin of the letters to the time of St. Irenæus. Harnack and his followers admit that Irenæus, the disciple of Polycarp, assigns the authorship to St. John the Apostle. St. Polycarp cites rather II John, 7, than I John, 4. St. Irenæus expressly quotes II John, 10, as the words of "John the Disciple of the Lord".

St. Clement of Alexandria speaks of the Epistles of John as do Origen and Eusebius. St John is telling us that we can all have that close intimate relationship with Jesus Christ. We have the witness of men who had direct and personal contact with Him.

The Gospel writers present their solid testimony on a historical reality. The form is that of an encyclical letter. Its destination is clearly the churches which St. John evangelized, he speaks to his "little children", "beloved", "brethren", and is affectionate and fatherly throughout the entire letter. The purpose is identical with the purpose of the Fourth Gospel -- that his children believe in Jesus Christ, the Son of God, and that believing have life eternal in His name (1 John 5:13; John 20:31).

John's letter was about the basics of faith in Christ. It helped his readers reflect honestly on their faith. If they loved one another, that was evidence of God's presence in their lives. But if they fought all the time or were selfish and did not look out for one another, they were betraying that they did not know God.

John describes love not as an emotion or feeling, but as obedience to the commandments of God. Jesus reiterated the importance of the commandments, the “greatest commandments,” ,love for God (Deuteronomy 6:5), and love for one another (Matthew 22:37-40; Leviticus 19:18).

The letter of 2 John is an urgent plea that the readers of John's letter should show their love for God and His son Jesus by obeying the commandment to love each other and live their lives in obedience to the Scriptures.

The book of 2 John is also a strong warning to be on the lookout for deceivers who were going about saying that Christ had not actually risen in the flesh. It is largely concerned with an urgent warning concerning deceivers who were not teaching the exact doctrine of Christ and who maintained that Jesus did not actually rise in the flesh but only spiritually. John is very anxious that true believers should be aware of these false teachers and have nothing to do with them.

St. John describes love not as an emotion or feeling, but as obedience to the commandments of God. Jesus reiterated the importance of the commandments, especially the “first and greatest commandment,” love for God (Deuteronomy 6:5) and the second—love for one another (Matthew 22:37-40; Leviticus 19:18).

St. John’s purpose in writing the 3rd letter was threefold. He writes to commend and encourage his beloved co-worker, Gaius, second, he indirectly warns and condemns the behavior of one Diotrephes, and third, he commends the example of Demetrius who was reported as having a good testimony from all.

Though some sources state that he was 94 when he died, others claim he was most likely 104. Traditionally, he is said to be the only apostle to die of natural causes. His tomb is located in Ephesus.

Summary Information:[52]

Letters of St. John

<u>I John</u>	
Chapters:	**5**
Verses:	**105**
<u>II John</u>	
Chapters:	**1**
Verses:	**13**
<u>III John</u>	
Chapters:	**1**
Verses:	**14**
OT Prophecies :	**0**
Verses of Prophecy (fulfilled):	**0**
Verses of Prophecy (unfulfilled):	**5**

52 ttp://en.wikipedia.org/wiki/Epistles_of_John

Course II (con't) , *1st Letter of St. John**
Suggested Reading Schedule and Discussion:

Week 5: Chapters 1 – 5

What does St. John say about some who claim to be without sin? What relation does sin have with salvation?

____

____

____

Can we love the world and still be a good Christian? Consider greatly successful philanthropists who are not Christian.

____

____

____

How do we recognize the Spirit of God? Are there other Spirits who are in warfare with the Christian Spirit of God?

____

____

____

* Space is provided for additional notations at the end of the course.

Course II (con't) , *2ndt Letter of St. John**
Suggested Reading Schedule and Discussion:

Week 5: Chapters 1

1. What was St. John's message to the chosen lady and her children? How does that relate today in our society?

Course II (con't) , *3rd Letter of St. John**
Suggested Reading Schedule and Discussion:

Week 5: Chapters 1

2. What was St. John's message of hospitality? Who should practice hospitality at all times?

---

* Space is provided for additional notations at the end of the course.

- *That which was from the beginning, which we have heard, which we have seen with our eyes, which we have looked at and our hands have touched—this we proclaim concerning the Word of life. [2]The life appeared; we have seen it and testify to it, and we proclaim to you the eternal life, which was with the Father and has appeared to us. We proclaim to you … And our fellowship is with the Father and with his Son, Jesus Christ.* (1 John 1-3)

- *"If we confess our sins, he is faithful and just and will forgive us our sins and purify us from all unrighteousness."* (1 John 1:9).

- *"Watch out that you do not lose what you have worked for, but that you may be rewarded fully. Anyone who runs ahead and does not continue in the teaching of Christ does not have God; whoever continues in the teaching has both the Father and the Son."* (2 John 8-9)[53]

---

53 http://www.gotquestions.org/Books-of-John.html

The End of Course Two

(Please jot down any additional notations which may be helpful in group discussions.)

Series IV. Course III
Revelation of St. John

Revelation 1:1,4,9 and 22:8 specifically identify the author of the book of Revelation as the apostle St. John. The book of Revelation was likely written between 90 and 95 AD from the Isle of Patmos.

The Revelation of Jesus Christ was given to St. John by God "to show his servants what must soon take place." This book is filled with mysteries about things to come. It is the final warning that the world will surely end and judgment will be certain. It gives us a tiny glimpse of heaven and all of the glories awaiting those who keep their robes white.

Revelation takes us through the great tribulation with all its woes and the final fire that all unbelievers will face for eternity. The book reiterates the fall of Satan and the doom he and his angels are bound for. We are shown the duties of all creatures and angels of heaven and the promises of the saints that live forever with Jesus.

The Revelation describes visions which proclaim for us the last days before Christ's return and the ushering in of the new heaven and new earth. It begins with letters to the seven churches of Asia Minor, then goes on to reveal the series of devastations poured out upon the earth; the mark of the beast, "666"; the climactic battle of Armageddon; the binding of Satan; the reign of the Lord; the Great White Throne Judgment; and the nature of the eternal city of God.

In Asia, Melito, Bishop of Sardis, one of the Seven Churches of the Apocalypse, acknowledged the Revelation of St. John and wrote a commentary on it (Eusebius, *Church History* IV.26). In Gaul, Irenaeus firmly believes in its Divine and Apostolic authority (*Against Heresies*

5.30). In Africa, Tertullian frequently quotes Revelation without apparent misgivings as to its authenticity (*Against Marcion* III). In Italy, Bishop Hippolytus assigns it to the Apostle St. John, and the Muratorian Fragment (a document about the beginning of the third century) enumerates it along with the other canonical writings.

The book of Revelation is culmination of the prophecies about the end times, beginning with the Old Testament. The description of the antichrist mentioned in Daniel 9:27 is developed fully in chapter 13 of Revelation. Outside of Revelation, examples of apocalyptic literature in the Bible are Daniel chapters 7-12, Isaiah chapters 24-27, Ezekiel chapters 37-41, and Zechariah chapters 9-12. All these prophecies come together in the book of Revelation.

Summary Information:[54]

Book of Revelation	
Chapters:	**22**
Verses:	**404**
OT Prophecies:	**0**
Verses of Prophecy (fulfilled):	**10**
Verses of Prophecy (unfulfilled):	**341**

54 ttp://en.wikipedia.org/wiki/Revelation_of_John

Course III, *Revelation of St. John**
Suggested Reading Schedule and Discussion:

Week 6: Chapters 1 –7

1. What are the 7 churches and the general message? Are these related to the churches of today? How?

___

___

___

2. Describe the throne in heaven. Discuss any symbolism that may come to mind. Who were the attendants on the throne and what were they saying in unison?

___

___

___

3. Who is the Lion of Judah, the Root of David, and the Lamb? Why is it He who broke the seals of the scroll?

___

___

___

* Space is provided for additional notations at the end of the course.

Course III, *Revelation of St. John**
Suggested Reading Schedule and Discussion:

Week 7: Chapters 8-14

1. Describe the 7 angels and the 7 trumpets. Discuss any symbolism that may come to mind.

___

___

___

2. Who are the woman, the dragon and the beast? To whom is their collective service?

___

___

___

3. What symbolism is there is the Lamb standing on Mt. Zion with the 144,000? Is this a remnant symbolism?

___

___

___

* Space is provided for additional notations at the end of the course.

Course III, *Revelation of St. John**
Suggested Reading Schedule and Discussion:

Week 8: Chapters 15-22

1. What are the 7 plagues? Discuss any symbolism that may come to mind. Does one see any relation to these plagues and the plagues of Egypt? Discuss.

2. Who is Babylon the Great? Discuss any symbolism that may come to mind. Is this relationship metaphorical or actual in our present day situation.

3. Describe the New Jerusalem. Notice the foundations had the names of the "12 Apostles of the Lamb". Who were, ultimately, the 12 Apostles. Discuss.

* Space is provided for additional notations at the end of the course.

- *He also forced everyone, small and great, …to receive a mark on his right hand or on his forehead, so that no one could buy or sell unless he had the mark, which is the name of the beast or the number of his name." (Revelation 13:16-17).*

- *"You are just in these judgments, you who are and who were, the Holy One, because you have so judged; for they have shed the blood of your saints and prophets, and you have given them blood to drink as they deserve. … Yes, Lord God Almighty, true and just are your judgments."(Revelation 16:5-7)*

- *"Then I saw a great white throne and Him who was seated on it. Earth and sky fled from his presence, and there was no place for them." (Revelation 20:11).*

- *Then I saw a new heaven and a new earth, for the first heaven and the first earth had passed away..(Revelation 21:1).*[55]

55 http://www.gotquestions.org/Revelation-of-John.html

The End of Course Three

(Please jot down any additional notations which may be helpful in group discussions.)

V. GENESIS SERIES

The foundational Old Testament books of Genesis, Exodus and Deuteronomy.

The first five books of the Holy Bible, the Pentateuch, or Torah, as it is called in the Judaist tradition, were traditionally written by Moses. It contains the foundational scriptures of the beginning of the world, God's beginning history with man, the journeys of God's chosen people of His covenant, Abraham, Isaac, and Jacob, and finishes with the creation of the Law.

Course One:	**The Book of Genesis**
Course Two:	**The Book of Exodus**
Course Three:	**The Book of Deuteronomy**

Series V. Course I
Book of Genesis

Traditionally, the first five books of the Holy Bible, the Pentateuch or Jewish Torah, were written by Moses. He specifically indicated that he was the author of the Book of Exodus (Exodus 17:14; 24:4-7; 34:27). The content of the books (oral tradition) dates between 1350 BC and 1400 BC. The oldest extant Biblical manuscripts (mss) of Genesis are the 24 fragments found among the Dead Sea Scrolls.

Many of the great questions of life are answered in Genesis. (1) Where did I come from? (God created us - Genesis 1:1) (2) Why am I here? (we are here to have a relationship with God - Genesis 15:6) (3) Where am I going? (we have a destination after death - Genesis 25:8). Genesis appeals to the scientist, the historian, the theologian, the housewife, the farmer, the traveler, and the man or woman of God. It is a fitting beginning for God's plan for mankind, the Bible.

The Book of Genesis is the "Book of Beginnings" in the Bible. Genesis, Greek for "Origins", recounts the Creation of all things in six literal 24-hour days, the Fall of Mankind and the Curse, the subsequent Worldwide Marine Cataclysm (Noah's Flood), the Dispersion at Babel, and finally the birth of the Jewish Nation.

Together, these events cover roughly 2,370 years of Earth's history. The Book of Genesis is divided into two principal sections: (i) Chapters 1-11 covers the Creation to the Dispersion and (ii) Chapters 12-50 covers the birth of Israel, from the calling of Abram (Abraham) until the death and burial of his great grandson Joseph in Egypt.

God chose Abraham, through whom He would create a chosen people and eventually the promised Messiah. The chosen line was passed on to Abraham's son Isaac, and then to Isaac's son Jacob. God changed Jacob's name to Israel, and his twelve sons became the ancestors of the twelve tribes of Israel.

Many New Testament themes have their roots in Genesis. Jesus Christ is the Seed of the woman who will destroy Satan's power (Gen. 3:15). As with Joseph, God's plan for the good of mankind through the sacrifice of His Son was intended for good, even though those who crucified Jesus intended it for evil.

For Jews, the theological importance of Genesis centers on the Covenants linking Yahweh (God) to his Chosen People and the people to the Promised Land. Christianity has reinterpreted Genesis as the prefiguration of Christian beliefs, specifically the Christian view of Christ as the fulfillment of the covenantal promises.

Many New Testament themes have their roots in Genesis. Jesus Christ is the Seed of the woman who will destroy Satan's power (Gen. 3:15). God always preserves a remnant of the faithful for Himself.

The remnant of Israelites returned to Jerusalem after the Babylonian captivity; God preserved a remnant through all the persecutions described in Isaiah and Jeremiah; a remnant of 7000 priests were hidden from the wrath of Jezebel; God promises that a remnant of Jews will one day embrace their true Messiah (Romans 11). The faith displayed by Abraham would be the gift of God and the basis of salvation for both Jew and Gentile (Ephesians 2:8-9; Hebrews 11).

Summary Information:[56]

Book of Genesis

Chapters	**50**
Verses:	**1533**
Verses of Prophecy (Fulfilled):	**123**
Verses of Prophecy (Unfulfilled):	**23**

Additional References and Peripheral Study Guides

- **Donald Guthrie, Eerdmans's Handbook to the Bible, (Grand Rapids: Eerdmans, 1973)**
- **Walter Eichrodt, Theology of the Old Testament, Vol. 1, (Philadelphia, Westminster, 1961)**
- **Walter Eichrodt, Theology of the Old Testament, Vol. 2, (Philadelphia, Westminster, 1967)**
- **Robert Huber, ED, The Bible through the Ages, (Pleasantville, Reader's Digest Association, 1989)**

[56]http://en.wikipedia.org/wiki/Book_of_Genesis

Course I, *Book of Genesis**
Suggested Reading Schedule and Discussion:

Week 1: Chapters 1 –7

1. Who wrote the first 5 books (the Pentateuch)? Reflect on the relationship of oral tradition and written tradition in this important foundational work.

___

___

___

2. How do we reconcile the archeological evidence which puts man at over 200,000 years in Africa yet the genealogy dating back to Adam is approximately 5,000 years? When did God create (approach?) mankind?

___

___

___

3. From where did Cain's wife suddenly appear? Was this story a regional or worldwide epic?

___

___

___

* Space is provided for additional notations at the end of the course.

Course I, *Book of Genesis**
Suggested Reading Schedule and Discussion:

Week 2: Chapters 8-14

1. What was God's covenant with Noah? Did God have other (different?) covenants with other Patriarchs?

____

____

____

2. Who were the 3 sons of Noah who "from them came all the peoples of the Earth". Discuss this genealogy.

____

____

____

3. How was Abraham "called"? Discuss the relationship of the sacrificial lamb to the sacrifice of Christ on the cross. What is our relationship to Isaac?

____

____

____

* Space is provided for additional notations at the end of the course.

Course I, *Book of Genesis**
Suggested Reading Schedule and Discussion:

Week 3: Chapters 15-21

1. What was God's covenant with Abraham? Why was a covenant required is God had made covenants with mankind previously?

____

____

____

2. What does the story of Hagar and Ishmael have to do with the current Islam and Arab nations? Reflect on this history and the relationship of God to Allah.

____

____

____

3. Why did God destroy Sodom and Gomorrah? Does this have any sociological meaning for us today?

____

____

____

* Space is provided for additional notations at the end of the course.

Course I, *Book of Genesis**
Suggested Reading Schedule and Discussion:

Week 4: Chapters 22 – 25, 49, 50

1. What did God do to test Abraham? Was Abraham willing or reluctant to be tested by God in this way?

____

____

____

2. Who were Jacob's (renamed Israel) sons? What relationships did they have with the future of Israel?

____

____

____

3. What did Jacob require of Joseph before his death? What does the bible say about the state of our death and bodily remain as related to the final resurrection?

____

____

____

* Space is provided for additional notations at the end of the course.

- *In the beginning God created the heavens and the earth…Then God said, "Let us make man in our image, in our likeness, and let them rule over the fish of the sea and the birds of the air, over the livestock, over all the earth, [and over all the creatures that move along the ground. So God created man in his own image, in the image of God he created him; male and female he created them.* (Genesis 1:1, 26-27)

- *By the sweat of your brow you will eat your food until you return to the ground, since from it you were taken; for dust you are and to dust you will return."* (Genesis 3:19)

- *"I will make you into a great nation and I will bless you; I will make your name great, and you will be a blessing. I will bless those who bless you, and whoever curses you I will curse; and all peoples on earth will be blessed through you."* (Genesis 12:2-3)

- *"You intended to harm me, but God intended it for good to accomplish what is now being done, the saving of many lives."* (Genesis 50:20)[57]

[57] http://www.gotquestions.org/Book-of-Genesis.html

The End of Course One

(Please jot down any additional notations which may be helpful in group discussions.)

Series V. Course II
Book of Exodus

Exodus (Greek: ἔξοδος, exodus, meaning "departure") or **Sh'moth** (Hebrew: שמות, literally "names", Modern Hebrew: Shmot) is the second of five books of the Torah/Pentateuch. Moses was the author of the Book of Exodus (Exodus 17:14; 24:4-7; 34:27).

Oral tradition places the contents of the book between 1350 BC and 1400 BC. Moses leads the Hebrews out of Egypt and through the wilderness to the Mountain of God: Mount Sinai. There Yahweh, through Moses, gives the Hebrews their laws and enters into a covenant with them, by which he will give them the land of Canaan in return for their faithfulness. The book ends with the construction of the Tabernacle.

Exodus begins where Genesis leaves off as God deals with His chosen people, the Jews. It traces the events from the time Israel entered Egypt as guests of Joseph, who was powerful in Egypt, until they were eventually delivered from the cruel bondage of slavery into which they had been brought by "...a new king...which knew not Joseph" (Exodus 1:8).

In God's timing, the exodus of the Israelites from Egypt marked the end of a period of oppression for Abraham's descendants (Genesis 15:13), and the beginning of the fulfillment of the covenant promise to Abraham that his descendants would not only live in the Promised Land, but would also multiply and become a great nation (Genesis 12:1-3, 7).

The purpose of the book may be expressed as tracing the rapid growth of Jacob's descendants from Egypt to the establishment of the theocratic nation in their Promised Land.

Chapters 1-14 describe the conditions of oppression of the Jews under Pharaoh, the rise of Moses as their deliverer, the plagues God brought upon Egypt for the refusal of their leader to submit to Him and the departure from Egypt. God's sovereign and powerful hand is seen in the miracles of the plagues.

The middle portion of Exodus (Chapters 15 – 25) is dedicated to the wandering in the wilderness and the miraculous provision by God for His people. But even though He gave them bread from heaven, sweet water from bitter, water from a rock, victory over those who would destroy them, His Law written on tablets of stone by His own hand, and His presence in the form of pillars of fire and cloud, the people continually grumbled and rebelled against Him.

Lastly, he commanded Moses to make the Tabernacle which would be used for the Jewish sacrifice to Yahweh until the coming of Christ.

The numerous sacrifices required of the Israelites were a picture of the ultimate sacrifice, the Passover Lamb of God, Jesus Christ. The night of the last plague on Egypt, an unblemished lamb was killed and its blood applied to the doorposts of the houses of God's people, protecting them from the angel of death. This foreshadowed Jesus, the Lamb of God without spot or blemish (1 Peter 1:19), whose blood applied to us ensures eternal life.

Among the symbolic presentations of Christ in the book of Exodus is the story of the water from the rock in Exodus 17:6. Just as Moses struck the rock to provide life-giving water for the people to drink, so did God strike the Rock of our salvation, crucifying Him for our sin, and from the Rock came the gift of living water (John 4:10). The provision of manna in the wilderness is a perfect picture of Christ, the Bread of Life (John 6:48)

Summary Information:[58]

Book of Exodus	
Chapters:	40
Verses:	1233
Verses of Prophecy (Fulfilled):	129
Verses of Prophecy (Unfulfilled):	2

58 http://en.wikipedia.org/wiki/Book_of_Exodus

Course II, *Book of Exodus**
Suggested Reading Schedule and Discussion:

Week 5: Chapters 1 –7

1. Why did the Egyptians enslave the Israelites? Was this a common practice among all of Egypt's adversaries?

---

2. How did God reveal Himself to Moses? Did Moses see Him face to face and walk with Him or was He hidden from view from all but Moses?

---

3. What part did Aaron play in the Israelite deliverance? Was he always true to Moses and his expectations?

---

* Space is provided for additional notations at the end of the course.

Course II, *Book of Exodus**
Suggested Reading Schedule and Discussion:

Week 6: Chapters 8-14

1. What were the plagues that came upon the Egyptians? Why did God harden Pharaoh's heart repeatedly?

____

____

____

2. Describe the ancient Egyptian Passover, the concept of the firstborn, and its current relation to Christianity .

____

____

____

3. Describe the Exodus from Egypt and the reason for the 40 year journey of the children of Israel into the promised land.

____

____

____

* Space is provided for additional notations at the end of the course.

Course II, *Book of Exodus**
Suggested Reading Schedule and Discussion:

Week 7: Chapters 15-21

1. What were the reasons for Manna and Quail? Did the Israelites receive the bounty gladly?

___

___

___

2. Who was Jethro and how did he advise Moses? How did Moses receive the advice and what was the result?

___

___

___

3. What are the 10 commandments? Did Jesus later confirm or deny those commands with His statements?

___

___

___

* Space is provided for additional notations at the end of the course.

Course II, *Book of Exodus**
Suggested Reading Schedule and Discussion:

Week 8: Chapters 22-25

1. Describe some of the more interesting property and social laws that God gave Moses for the Israelites.

___

___

___

2. What were the 3 Annual Festivals? Do the Israelites observe these ancient customs today? Why?

___

___

___

3. How did God confirm His covenant with Moses? After a covenant with Noah and Abraham, Isaac and Jacob, why did he make a covenant with Moses?

___

___

___

* Space is provided for additional notations at the end of the course.

- *These are the names of the sons of Israel who went to Egypt with Jacob, each with his family: Reuben, Simeon, Levi and Judah; Issachar, Zebulun and Benjamin; Dan and Naphtali; Gad and Asher. The descendants of Jacob numbered seventy in all; Joseph was already in Egypt (Exodus 1:1-5)*

- *'Then a new king, who did not know about Joseph, came to power in Egypt." (Exodus 1:8)*

- *"God heard their groaning and he remembered his covenant with Abraham, with Isaac and with Jacob. So God looked on the Israelites and was concerned about them."*
  (Exodus 2:24-25)

- *'It is the Passover sacrifice to the LORD, who passed over the houses of the Israelites in Egypt and spared our homes when he struck down the Egyptians.'" Then the people bowed down and worshiped." (Exodus 12:27)*[59]

[59] http://www.gotquestions.org/Book-of-Exodus.html

The End of Course Two

(Please jot down any additional notations which may be helpful in group discussions.)

Series V. Course III
Book of Deuteronomy

The sermons in Deuteronomy were in fact a collection of Moses' sermons to Israel just before they crossed the Jordan: "These are the words which Moses spoke" (1:1) They were given during the 40-day period prior to Israel's entering the Promised Land.

The first sermon was delivered on the 1st day of the 11th month (1:3), and the Israelites crossed the Jordan 70 days later, on the 10th day of the 1st month (Joshua 4:19). Subtract 30 days of mourning after Moses' death (Deuteronomy 34:8), and we're left with 40 days. Oral tradition places the contents of the book at 1410 BC.

The book of Deuteronomy was given to remind them of God's law and God's power. Many New Testament themes are present in the Book of Deuteronomy. The foremost among them is the necessity of keeping perfectly the Mosaic Law and the impossibility of doing so. The endless sacrifices necessary to atone for the sins of the people—who continually transgressed the Law—would find their fulfillment in the final "once for all" sacrifice of Christ (Hebrews 10:10). Because of His atoning work on the cross, we would need no further sacrifices for sin.

God's choosing of the Israelites as His special people foreshadows His choosing of those who would believe in Christ (1 Peter 2:9). In Deuteronomy 18:15-19, Moses prophesies of another prophet—the ultimate Prophet to come who is the Messiah. Like Moses, He would receive and preach divine revelation and He would lead His people (John 6:14 ; 7:40).

A few of the laws which were given in the book of Deuteronomy:

- The worship of God must remain pure, uninfluenced by neighboring cultures and their 'idolatrous' religious practices. The death penalty is prescribed for conversion from Yahwism and for proselytization.
- The law of rape prescribes various conditions and penalties, depending on whether the girl is engaged to be married or not, and whether the rape occurs in town or in the country. (Deuteronomy 22)
- A regular Jubilee Year during which all debts are cancelled.
- Yahwistic religious festivals—including Passover...are part of Israel's worship
- The offices of Judge, King, Kohen (temple priest), and Prophet are instituted.
- Rules which regulate marriage, and allow divorce.
- Regulations for ritual cleanliness and general hygiene.
- A ban on religious prostitution, homosexuality and transvestitism.

The Israelites are commanded to remember four things: God's faithfulness, God's holiness, God's blessings, and God's warnings. The first three chapters recap the trip from Egypt to their current location, Moab. Chapter 4 is a call to obedience, to be faithful to the God Who was faithful to them. Chapters 5 through 26 are a repetition of the law. The Ten Commandments, the laws concerning sacrifices and specials days, and the rest of the law are given to the new generation.

Deuteronomy records the death of Moses. He renews the covenant between God and the Israelites. By the direction of YHWH (the Hebrew most sacred name for God), Moses then appoints Joshua as his heir to lead the people into Canaan. He writes down the law and gives it to the Priests, commanding them to read it before all Israel at the end of every seven years, during the Feast of Booths.

A new generation of Israelites was about to enter the Promised Land. This multitude had not experienced the miracle at the Red Sea or heard the law given at Sinai, and they were about to enter a new land with many dangers and temptations.

Summary Information:[60]

Book of Deuteronomy	
Chapters:	**34**
Verses:	**958**
Verses of Prophecy (Fulfilled):	**230**
Verses of Prophecy (Unfulfilled):	**37**

60 http://en.wikipedia.org/wiki/Book_of_Deuteronomy

Course III, *Book of Deuteronomy**
Suggested Reading Schedule and Discussion:

Week 9: Chapters 1 – 6, 17

1. Why was the Lord angry with the Israelites and did He ultimately prevent Moses from entering Canaan?

____

____

____

2. What was forbidden of the Israelites? Was God specific in His admonishments to the Jews: Through whom did He speak?

____

____

____

3. What was God's command regarding the court of law? Do these general criteria for laws exist today ?

____

____

____

* Space is provided for additional notations at the end of the course.

Course III, *Book of Deuteronomy**
Suggested Reading Schedule and Discussion:

Week 10: Chapters 18 – 24

1. How did God provide for priests and Levites? Do the Jews of today observe similar laws for its priests?

____

____

____

2. Discuss some of the more interesting social laws. Relate some of these to our modern society.

____

____

____

3. How could one be excluded from the assembly? Was it possible for one to come back into the fellowship?

____

____

____

* Space is provided for additional notations at the end of the course.

Course III, *Book of Deuteronomy**
Suggested Reading Schedule and Discussion:

Week 11: Chapters 25 – 31

1. Discuss God 's commandment to tithe. Is this the strict or general rule for only Judaism or Christianity? Why?

____

____

____

2. Discuss the more interesting 'curses' from God. Were these curses only for the Israelites or others as well?

____

____

____

3. Who was to succeed Moses? How old was he when he died and what was the mission after Moses?

____

____

____

* Space is provided for additional notations at the end of the course.

Course III, *Book of Deuteronomy**
Suggested Reading Schedule and Discussion:

Week 12: Chapters 32 – 34

1. Where exactly was Moses buried? Why is this fact important or unimportant in Jewish history?

____

____

____

2. Which tribe received the greatest blessing from Moses. Why was it important to receive a blessing?

____

____

____

3. How did Moses compare with all of the other prophets in Israel? Was he a reluctant or aggressive prophet?

____

____

____

* Space is provided for additional notations at the end of the course.

- *"Do not add to what I command you and do not subtract from it, but keep the commands of the LORD your God that I give you." (Deuteronomy 4:2)*

- *Hear, O Israel: The LORD our God, the LORD is one. Love the LORD your God with all your heart and with all your soul and with all your strength. These commandments that I give you today are to be upon your hearts. Impress them on your children. Talk about them when you sit at home and when you walk along the road, when you lie down and when you get up." (Deuteronomy 6:4-7)*

- *He said to them, 'Take to heart all the words I have solemnly declared to you this day, so that you may command your children to obey carefully all the words of this law. They are not just idle words for you—they are your life. By them you will live long in the land you are crossing the Jordan to possess." (Deuteronomy 32:46-47)*[61]

[61] http://www.gotquestions.org/Book-of-Deuteronomy.html

The End of Course Three

(Please jot down any additional notations which may be helpful in group discussions.)

VI. MAJOR PROPHETS SERIES

The prophetic books of Isaiah, Ezekiel, Jeremiah, Daniel, and Psalms.

The major prophets of the Old Testament, including those in this series, bear witness to the "stiff-necked and obstinate" people Israel and contain hundreds of prophecies of the coming Messiah which were foretold many centuries before Jesus the Christ walked on the Earth.

Course One:	**The Book of the Prophet Isaiah** **The Book of the Prophet Ezekiel**
Course Two:	**The Book of the Prophet Jeremiah** **The Book of the Prophet Daniel**
Course Three:	**The Book of Psalms**

Series VI. Course I
Book of Isaiah

Isaiah 1:1 identifies the author of the Book of Isaiah as the Prophet Isaiah. The Book of Isaiah was written between 701 and 681 BC. He lived in the late eighth century BC and was part of the upper class but urged care of the downtrodden. At the end, he was loyal to King Hezekiah, but disagreed with the King's attempts to forge alliances with Egypt and Babylon in response to the Assyrian threat.

Isaiah prophesied during the reigns of four kings: Uzziah (also known as Azariah), Jotham, Ahaz, and Hezekiah. According to tradition, he was martyred during the reign of Manasseh, who came to the throne in 687 BC, by being cut in two by a wooden saw. He is described as having access to the kings would suggest an aristocratic origin.

The 66 chapters of Isaiah consist primarily of prophecies of Babylon, Assyria, Philistia, Moab, Syria, Israel (the northern kingdom), Ethiopia, Egypt, Arabia, and Phoenicia.

The prophesies concerning them can be summarized as saying that God is the God of the whole earth, and that nations which think of themselves as secure in their own power might well be conquered by other nations, at God's command.

More than any other book in the Old Testament, Isaiah focuses on the salvation that will come through the Messiah. The Messiah will one day rule in justice and righteousness (Isaiah 9:7; 32:1). The reign of the Messiah will bring peace and safety to Israel (Isaiah 11:6-9).

Through the Messiah, Israel will be a light to all the nations (Isaiah 42:6; 55:4-5). The Messiah's kingdom on earth (Isaiah chapter 65-66) is the goal towards which all of the Book of Isaiah points. It is during the reign of the Messiah that God's righteousness will be fully revealed to the world.

The Book of Isaiah presents our Savior to us in undeniable detail. He is the only way to heaven, the only means of obtaining the grace of God, the only Way, the only Truth, and the only Life (John 14:6; Acts 4:12).

Chapter 53 of Isaiah describes the coming Messiah and the suffering that He would endure in order to pay for our sins. In His sovereignty, God orchestrated every detail of the crucifixion to fulfill every prophecy of this chapter, as well as all other messianic prophecies of the Old Testament.

Isaiah contains a complete picture of the Gospel. Jesus was despised and rejected (v. 3; Luke 13:34; John 1:10-11), stricken by God (v.4; Matthew 27:46), and pierced for our transgressions (v. 5; John 19:34; 1 Peter 2:24). By His suffering, He paid the punishment we deserved and became for us the ultimate and perfect sacrifice (v. 5; Hebrews 10:10).

The Book of Isaiah presents our Savior to us as the only way to heaven, the only means of obtaining the grace of God, the only Way, the only Truth, and the only Life (John 14:6; Acts 4:12).

Knowing the price Christ paid for us, how can we neglect or reject "so great a salvation"? (Hebrews 2:3). We have only a few, short years on earth to come to Christ and embrace the salvation only He offers. There is no second chance after death and eternity in hell is a long time.

Summary Information:[62]

Book of Isaiah	
Chapters:	**66**
Verses:	**1292**
Verses of Prophecy (Fulfilled):	**634**
Verses of Prophecy (Unfulfilled):	**395**

Additional References and Peripheral Study Guides

- **Sir George Adam Smith, The Book of Isaiah, vol. 2, (New York: Harper & Row, 1965)**
- **John Bright, Jeremiah, (New York: Doubleday publishers, 1965)**
- **Walther Eichrodt, Theology of the Old Testament, Vol. 1, (Philadelphia, Westminster, 1961)**
- **Walther Eichrodt, Theology of the Old Testament, Vol. 2, (Philadelphia, Westminster, 1967)**

62 http://en.wikipedia.org/wiki/Book_of_Isaiah

Course I, *Book of Isaiah**
Suggested Reading Schedule and Discussion:

Week 1: Chapters 1 – 7

1. What was the King attempting to do which prompted Isaiah's prophecies? What was the result?

___

___

___

2. Which was the more rebellious region in Israel (Judah or Galilee)? Did Isaiah prophesy to both of them?

___

___

___

3. What was the sign of Immanuel? How does the name 'Jesus' connect to this ancient name for the Messiah?

___

___

___

* Space is provided for additional notations at the end of the course.

Course I, *Book of Isaiah**
Suggested Reading Schedule and Discussion:

Week 2: Chapters 8 – 14

1. What were the two nations which Isaiah prophesied against? Did Isaiah also go into bondage?

___

___

___

2. Why was Jerusalem going to get the same treatment that God had judged against the Samaritans? What was crime and curse from God on the Samaritans?

___

___

___

3. What child is born and what names will they call him? How are these related to the Christ-child and Messiah?

___

___

___

* Space is provided for additional notations at the end of the course.

Course I, *Book of Isaiah**
Suggested Reading Schedule and Discussion:

Week 3: Chapters 47 – 53

1. Who is the "Servant of the Lord"? Is this title used in the Old and New Testaments?

___

___

___

2. These chapters, particularly chapter 63, portray the Messiah more emphatically than perhaps anywhere in the Bible. Reflect on the specific Messianic promises.

___

___

___

3. Discuss the Suffering and Glory of the Servant. How is this Servant related to Jesus Christ?

___

___

___

* Space is provided for additional notations at the end of the course.

- *"Therefore the Lord himself will give you a sign: The virgin (maiden) will be with child and will give birth to a son, and will call him Immanuel." (Isaiah 7:14)*

- *For to us a child is born, to us a son is given … He will reign on David's throne and over his kingdom, establishing and upholding it with justice and righteousness from that time on and forever. The zeal of the LORD almighty will accomplish this." (Isaiah 9:6-7)*

- *"How you have fallen from heaven, O morning star, son of the dawn! You have been cast down to the earth, you who once laid low the nations! "I will ascend to heaven; I will raise my throne above the stars of God; I will sit enthroned on the mount of assembly, on the utmost heights of the sacred mountain." (Isaiah 14:12-13)*

- *But he was pierced for our transgressions, he was crushed for our iniquities; … by his wounds we are healed. each of us has turned to his own way; and the LORD has laid on him the iniquity of us all." (Isaiah 53:5-6)*[63]

---

[63] http://www.gotquestions.org/Book-of-Isaiah.html

Series VI. Course I (con't)
Book of Ezekiel

Ezekiel (pron.: /ɨˈziːki.əl/; Hebrew: יְחֶזְקֵאל, *Y'ḥez'qel*, Hebrew pronunciation: [jəħezˈqel]), Arabic:حزقيال *Hazqiyal*, 'God will strengthen' (from **חזק**, *ḥazaq*, [ħaˈzaq], literally 'to fasten upon,' figuratively 'strong,' and **אל**, *el*, [ʔel], literally 'God', and so figuratively 'The Almighty') is the central protagonist of the Book of Ezekiel in the Hebrew BibleHe was a contemporary of both Jeremiah and Daniel.

Date of Writing: The Book of Ezekiel was likely written between 593 and 565 B.C. during the Babylonian captivity of the Jews. Isaiah 1:1

Ezekiel ministered to his generation who were both exceedingly sinful and thoroughly hopeless. By means of his prophetic ministry he attempted to bring them to immediate repentance and to confidence in the distant future. He taught that: (1) God works through human messengers; (2) Even in defeat and despair God's people need to affirm God's sovereignty; (3) God's Word never fails; (4) God is present and can be worshiped anywhere; (5) People must obey God if they expect to receive blessings; and (6) God's Kingdom will come.

Ezekiel 34 is the chapter wherein God denounces the leaders of Israel as false shepherds for their poor care of His people. Instead of caring for the sheep of Israel, they cared for themselves. They ate well, were well-clothed and well-cared for by the very people they had been placed over (Ezekiel 34:1-3).

By contrast, Jesus is the Good Shepherd who lays down His life for the sheep and who protects them from the wolves who would destroy the flock (John 10:11-12).

Verse 4 of chapter 34 describes people whom the shepherds failed to minister to as weak, sick, injured and lost. Jesus is the Great Physician who heals our spiritual wounds (Isaiah 53:5) by His death on the cross. He is the one who seeks and saves that which is lost (Luke 19:10)

Ezekiel's book can be divided into four sections:

- Chapters 1-24: prophecies on the ruin of Jerusalem
- Chapters 25-32: prophecies of God's judgment on nearby nations
- Chapter 33: a last call for repentance to Israel
- Chapters 34-48: prophecies concerning the future restoration of Israel

In July 592 BC, at the age of 30, Ezekiel describes his calling to be a prophet, by going into great detail about his encounter with God who rode upon a chariot of four wheels guided by Cherubs. For the next five years he incessantly prophesied the destruction of Jerusalem and its temple, which was met with some opposition and drama.

However, Ezekiel and his contemporaries like Jeremiah, another prophet who was living in Jerusalem at that time, witnessed the fulfillment of their prophecies when Jerusalem was finally sacked by the Babylonians. The date of the sacking, 587 BC, is confirmed by Babylonian cuneiform records discovered by archeologists.

Summary Information:[64]

Book of Ezekiel

Chapters:	**48**
Verses:	**1273**
Verses of Prophecy (Fulfilled):	**530**
Verses of Prophecy (Unfulfilled):	**433**

64 http://en.wikipedia.org/wiki/Book_of_Ezekiel

Course I (con't), *Book of Ezekiel**
Suggested Reading Schedule and Discussion:

Week 4: Chapters 1 – 7

1. What was Ezekiel's vision of the Living Creatures? How is that related to the Christ message

___

___

___

2. Why was Ezekiel called to prophecy against the Israelites? What were the results?

___

___

___

3. What did he mean by his prophecy on "the end has come"? What happened to Israel and did they return?

___

___

___

* Space is provided for additional notations at the end of the course.

Course I (con't), *Book of Ezekiel**
Suggested Reading Schedule and Discussion:

Week 5: Chapters 18, 28, 33, 48

1. What happens to the soul who sins? How does Judaism and Christianity agree on this concept?

___

___

___

2. Why was Ezekiel called a "Watchman"? What other names could be attributed to his service?

___

___

___

3. What were the tribes of Israel and how were they divided? (Refer to map in Bible if available)

___

___

___

* Space is provided for additional notations at the end of the course.

- *He said: ' I am sending you to the Israelites, to a rebellious nation that has rebelled against me; they and their fathers have been in revolt against me to this very day. The people to whom I am sending you are obstinate and stubborn. "This is what the Sovereign LORD says." And whether they listen or fail to listen - for they are a rebellious house - they will know that a prophet has been among them.'"(Ezekiel 2:3-6),*

- *"'You were the model of perfection, full of wisdom and perfect in beauty. You were in Eden, the garden of God; every precious stone...Your settings and mountings were made of gold; on the day you were created they were prepared. You were anointed as a guardian cherub, for so I ordained you. You were on the holy mount of God; you walked among the fiery stones." (Ezekiel 28:12-14)*

- *"Say to them, 'As surely as I live, declares the Sovereign LORD, I take no pleasure in the death of the wicked, but rather that they turn from their ways and live. Turn! Turn from your evil ways! Why will you die, O house of Israel?' (Ezekiel 33:11)*[65]

65 http://www.gotquestions.org/Book-of-Ezekiel.html

The End of Course One

(Please jot down any additional notations which may be helpful in group discussions.)

Series VI. Course II
Book of Jeremiah

Jeremiah chapter 1, verse 1 identifies the Prophet Jeremiah as the author of the Book of Jeremiah. The Book of Jeremiah was written between 630 and 580 BC. It was originally written in a complex and poetic Hebrew (apart from verse 10:11, curiously written in Biblical Aramaic), recording the words and events surrounding the life of the Jewish prophet Jeremiah who lived at the time of the destruction of Solomon's Temple (587-586 BC) in Jerusalem during the fall of the Kingdom of Judah at the hands of Babylonia.

According to the book, the Prophet Jeremiah was a son of a priest from Anatot in the land of Benjamin, who lived in the last years of the Kingdom of Judah just prior to, during, and immediately after the siege of Jerusalem, culminating in the destruction of the temple.

The Book of Jeremiah is primarily a message of judgment on Judah for rampant idolatry (Jeremiah 7:30-34; 16:10-13; 22:9; 32:29; 44:2-3). After the death of King Josiah, the last righteous king, the nation of Judah had almost completely abandoned God and His commandments. Jeremiah compares Judah to a prostitute (Jeremiah 2:20; 3:1-3).

Jeremiah was warning Judah that God's judgment was at hand. God had delivered Judah from destruction on countless occasions, but His mercy was at its end. Jeremiah records King Nebuchadnezzar conquering Judah and making it subject to him (Jeremiah 24:1).

After further rebellion, God brought Nebuchadnezzar and the Babylonian armies back to destroy and desolate Judah and Jerusalem (Jeremiah chapter 52). Even in this most severe judgment, God promises restoration of Judah back into the land God has given them (Jeremiah 29:10).

The Prophet Jeremiah had a most difficult message to deliver. Jeremiah loved Judah, but he loved God much more. As painful as it was for Jeremiah to deliver a consistent message of judgment to his own people, Jeremiah was obedient to what God told him to do and say. Jeremiah hoped and prayed for mercy from God for Judah, but also trusted that God was good, just, and righteous.

According to the book, for a quarter century prior to the destruction, Jeremiah repeatedly issued prophecies predicting God's forthcoming judgment; advocating the Jews put down idols and repent in hopes of turning away God's judgment and destiny as chosen people.

In the final analysis, Jeremiah's fellow Jews refused to heed his warnings and did not repent. His efforts failed and he witnessed the destruction of everything he knew, the Jewish exile of the elite to Babylonia.

Parts of the Book of Jeremiah have been found among the Dead Sea Scrolls in cave 4 in Qumran. These texts, in Hebrew, correspond both to the Masoretic Text and the Septuagint Text. The Septuagint (Greek or 'LXX') version of this book is, in its arrangement and in other particulars, different from the Masoretic Hebrew. Note that the Septuagint does not include 10:6-8; 25:14; 27:19-22; 29:16-20; 33:14-26; 39:4-13; 52:2, 3, 15, 28-30.

Jeremiah 23:5-6 presents a prophecy of the coming Messiah, Jesus Christ. The prophet describes Him as a Branch from the house of David (v. 5; Matthew 1), the King who would reign in wisdom and righteousness (v. 5, Revelation 11:15). It is Christ who will finally be recognized by Israel as her true Messiah as He provides salvation for chosen ones (v. 6; Romans 11:26)

Summary Information:[66]

Book of Jeremiah	
Chapters:	**52**
Verses:	**1364**
Verses of Prophecy (Fulfilled):	**666**
Verses of Prophecy (Unfulfilled):	**180**

66 http://en.wikipedia.org/wiki/Book_of_Jeremiah

Course II, *Book of Jeremiah**
Suggested Reading Schedule and Discussion:

Week 6: Chapters 11 – 17

1. Against what and primarily where did Jeremiah prophecy? What were the results?

___

___

___

2. Why was the covenant broken? Discuss other covenants that God made with His chosen people.

___

___

___

3. Describe linen belt and wineskins in Jeremiah's prophecies. How are they used as metaphors?

___

___

___

* Space is provided for additional notations at the end of the course.

Course II, *Book of Jeremiah**
Suggested Reading Schedule and Discussion:

Week 6: Chapters 18 – 23

1. Describe the significance of the Potter's house. How does that relate to the Christian experience?

___

___

___

2. What was Zedekiah's request? What relationship did he have with Jeremiah and what were the results?

___

___

___

3. What is the name of the righteous branch and what is His relation to Israel ? How does Jesus relate to these passages in His ministry in the New Testament?

___

___

___

* Space is provided for additional notations at the end of the course.

- *"Before I formed you in the womb I knew you, before you were born I set you apart; I appointed you as a prophet to the nations." (Jeremiah 1:5)*

- *"The heart is deceitful above all things and beyond cure. Who can understand it?" (Jeremiah 17:9)*

- *The days are coming," declares the LORD, when I will raise up to David a righteous Branch, a King who will reign wisely and do what is just and right in the land. In his days Judah will be saved and Israel will live in safety. This is the name by which he will be called: The LORD Our Righteousness (Jeremiah 23:5-6)*

- *"This is what the LORD says: 'When seventy years are completed for Babylon, I will come to you and fulfill my gracious promise to bring you back to this place, for I know the plans I have for you,' declares the LORD, 'plans to prosper you and not to harm you, plans to give you hope and a future.'" (Jeremiah 29:10-11)*[67]

---

67 http://www.gotquestions.org/Book-of-Jeremiah.html

Series VI. Course II (con't)
Book of Daniel

The Book of Daniel identifies the Prophet Daniel as its author (Daniel 9:2; 10:2). Jesus mentions Daniel as the author as well (Matthew 24:15). The Book of Daniel was likely written between 540 and 530 BC. Originally written in Hebrew and Aramaic, it is set during the Babylonian Captivity, a period when Jews were deported and exiled to Babylon following the Siege of Jerusalem of 597 BC.

Daniel, an Israelite, becomes an adviser to Nebuchadnezzar, the ruler of Babylon from 605 to 562 BC. In 605 BC, Nebuchadnezzar King of Babylon had conquered Judah and deported many of its inhabitants to Babylon – Daniel included.

Daniel served in the royal court of Nebuchadnezzar and several rulers who followed Nebuchadnezzar. The Book of Daniel records the actions, prophecies, and visions of the Prophet Daniel.

The book has two distinct parts: a series of six narratives (chapters one to six) and four apocalyptic visions (chapters seven to twelve). The narratives take the form of court stories which focus on tests of religious fidelity involving Daniel and his friends (chapters one, three and six), and Daniel's interpretation of royal dreams and visions (chapters two, four and five).

Chapter 1 describes the conquest of Jerusalem by the Babylonians. Along with many others, Daniel and his three friends were deported to Babylon and because of their courage and the obvious blessings of God upon them, they were "promoted" in the king's service (Daniel 1:17-20). Chapters 2-7 record Nebuchadnezzar having a dream that only Daniel could correctly interpret. Nebuchadnezzar's dream of a great statue represented the kingdoms that would arise in the future. Nebuchadnezzar made a great statue of himself and forced everyone to worship it. Shadrach, Meshach, and Abednego refused and were miraculously spared by God despite being thrown into a fiery furnace. Nebuchadnezzar is judged by God for his pride, but later restored once he recognized and admitted God's sovereignty.

Daniel chapter 5 records Nebuchadnezzar's son Belshazzar misusing the items taken from the Temple in Jerusalem and receiving a message from God, written into the wall, in response. Only Daniel could interpret the writing, a message of coming judgment from God. Daniel is thrown into the lions' den for refusing to pray to the emperor, but was miraculously spared. God gave Daniel a vision of four beasts. The four beasts represented the kingdoms of Babylon, Medo-Persia, Greece, and Rome.

We see in the stories of the fiery furnace and Daniel in the lions' den a foreshadowing of the salvation provided by Christ. The three men declare that God is a saving God who can provide a way of escape from the (Daniel 3:17). In the same way, by sending Jesus to die for our sins, God has provided an escape from the fires of hell (1 Peter 3:18). In Daniel's case, God provided an angel to shut the lions' mouths and saved Daniel from death. Jesus Christ is our provision from the dangers of the sin that threatens to consume us.

Daniel's vision of the end times depicts Israel's Messiah by whom many will be made pure and holy (Daniel 12:10). He is our righteousness (1 Peter 5:21) by whom our sins, though blood-red, will be washed away and we will be as white as snow (Isaiah 1:18).

When Nebuchadnezzar threw Shadrach, Meshach and Abednego into the fiery furnace for not bowing down and worshipping him, Daniel records his reaction: Then King Nebuchadnezzar leaped to his feet in amazement and asked his advisers, "Weren't there three men that we tied up and threw into the fire?" They replied, "Certainly, O king." (Daniel 3:25) He said, **"Look! I see *four men* walking around in the fire, unbound and unharmed, and the fourth looks like a son of the gods."** (Daniel 3:26). Some evangelical Christians believe the "4th man" was the Christ, the son of God.

Summary Information:[68]

Book of Daniel	
Chapters:	**12**
Verses:	**357**
Verses of Prophecy (Fulfilled):	**79**
Verses of Prophecy (Unfulfilled):	**60**

[68] http://en.wikipedia.org/wiki/Book_of_Daniel

Course II (con't) , *Book of Daniel*
Suggested Reading Schedule and Discussion:

Week 7: Chapters 1 – 7

1. What was Nebuchadnezzar's dream and how did Daniel interpret? What were the results?

___

___

___

2. Why were Shadrach, Messhach, and Abednego thrown into the fiery furnace and what happened? Who is the '4th man' according to Christology?

___

___

___

3. How many men did Nebuchadnezzar see in the fiery furnace? How do you respond to this discrepancy?

___

___

___

* Space is provided for additional notations at the end of the course.

Course II (con't) , *Book of Daniel*
Suggested Reading Schedule and Discussion:

Week 8: Chapters 8 – 12

1. What was Daniels vision of a Ram and Goat? How did these relate in his prophecies?

___

___

___

2. What were the "Seventy Sevens" and in what context did they occur?

___

___

___

3. Discuss Daniel's famous prophecy of the end times. How do we relate this time-specific prophecy to the evolution of our modern society?

___

___

___

* Space is provided for additional notations at the end of the course.

- *The king talked with them, and he found none equal to Daniel, Hananiah, Mishael and Azariah ; so they entered the king's service. In every matter of wisdom and understanding about which the king questioned them, he found them ten times better than all the magicians and enchanters in his whole kingdom." (Daniel 1:19-20)*

- *"If we are thrown into the blazing furnace, the God we serve is able to save us from it and he will rescue us from your hand, O king, but even if he does not, we want you to know, O king, that we will not serve your gods or worship the image of gold you have set up." (Daniel 3:17-18)*

- *Know and understand this: From the issuing of the decree to restore and rebuild Jerusalem until the Anointed One, the ruler, comes, there will be seven 'sevens,' and sixty-two 'sevens.' ... The end will come like a flood: War will continue until the end, and desolations have been decreed. He will confirm a covenant with many for one 'seven.' In the middle of the 'seven' he will put an end to sacrifice and offering. And on a wing [of the temple] he will set up an abomination that causes desolation, until the end that is decreed is poured out on him." (Daniel 9:25-27)"*[69]

[69] http://www.gotquestions.org/Book-of-Daniel.html

The End of Course Two

(Please jot down any additional notations which may be helpful in group discussions.)

Series VI. Course III

Book of Psalms

Psalms (Hebrew: Tehilim, תהילים, or "praises") is a book of the Hebrew Bible in the collected works known as the "Writings" or Ketuvim. In Islam, it is called the Zabur of Dāwud, or the *Psalms of David.* It is clear that the 150 individual psalms were written by many different people across a period of a thousand years in Israel's history. They must have been compiled and put together in their present form by some unknown editor shortly after the captivity ended about 537 B.C.

The brief descriptions that introduce the psalms have David listed as author in 73 instances. David's personality and identity are clearly stamped on many of these psalms. David is definitely not the author of the entire collection. The Book of Psalms is the longest book in the Bible, with 150 individual psalms. The psalms deal with such subjects as God and His creation, war, worship, wisdom, sin and evil, judgment, justice, and the coming of the Messiah.

Two of the psalms (72) and (127) are attributed to Solomon, David's son and successor. Psalm 90 is a prayer assigned to Moses. Another group of 12 psalms (50) and (73—83) is ascribed to the family of Asaph. The sons of Korah wrote 11 psalms (42, 44-49, 84-85,87-88). Psalm 88 is attributed to Heman, while (89) is assigned to Ethan the Ezrahite. With the exception of Solomon and Moses, all these additional authors were priests or Levites who were responsible for providing music for sanctuary worship during David's reign.

Fifty of the psalms designate no specific person as author. The oldest psalm in the collection is probably the prayer of Moses (90), a reflection on the frailty of man as compared to the eternity of God. The latest psalm is probably (137), a song of lament clearly written during the days when the Hebrews were being held captive by the Babylonians, from about 586 to 538 BC.

When the Bible was divided into chapters, each Psalm was assigned its own chapter. Psalms are sometimes referenced as chapters, despite chapter assignments postdating the initial composition of the "canonical" Psalms by at least 1,500 years. The organization and numbering of the Psalms differs slightly between the (Masoretic) Hebrew and the (Septuagint) Greek manuscripts.

The Book of Psalms is divided into 5 books:

1. The first book comprises the first 41 Psalms. While Davidic authorship cannot be confirmed, this probably is the oldest section of the Psalms.
2. The second book consists of the next 31 Psalms . Eighteen of these are ascribed to David. Psalm 72 is traditionally understood as being written by David as a prayer for his son. The rest are anonymous.
3. The third book contains seventeen Psalms. Psalm 86 is ascribed to David, Psalm 88 to Heman, and Psalm 89 to Ethan the Ezrahite.
4. The fourth book also contains seventeen Psalms (90–106), of which Psalm 90 is ascribed to Moses, and Psalms 101 and 103 to David
5. The fifth book contains the remaining 44 Psalms. Of these, 15 are ascribed to David, one (Psalm 127) as a charge to Solomon.

God's provision of a Savior for His people is a recurring theme in the Psalms. Prophetic pictures of the Messiah are seen in numerous psalms. Psalm 2:1-12 portrays the Messiah's triumph and kingdom. Psalm 16:8-11 foreshadows His death and resurrection. Psalm 22 shows us the suffering Savior on the cross and presents detailed prophecies of the crucifixion, all of which were fulfilled perfectly.

Most manuscripts of the Septuagint also include a Psalm 151, present in Eastern Orthodox translations; a Hebrew version of this poem was found in the *Psalms Scroll* of the Dead Sea Scrolls. God's provision of a Savior for His people is a recurring theme in the Psalms.

Summary Information:[70]

Book of Psalms	
Chapters:	**150**
Verses:	**2461**
Verses of Prophecy (Fulfilled):	**160**
Verses of Prophecy (Unfulfilled):	**274**

[70] http://en.wikipedia.org/wiki/Book_of_Psalms

Course III, *Book of Psalms**
Suggested Reading Schedule and Discussion:

Week 9: Chapters 1 – 7

1. Who were the prophets in the largest book of the Bible, the Psalms? Which prophet wrote the greatest majority of Psalms and which one wrote the oldest.

____

____

____

2. On what is David asking the Lord to judge him? Does he waver throughout the psalms from confident to fearful and back again? Relate that to today's society.

____

____

____

3. Why is man called "Blessed"? According to Christ and the Christian doctrine, who is worthy to be called this?

____

____

____

* Space is provided for additional notations at the end of the course.

Course III, *Book of Psalms**

Suggested Reading Schedule and Discussion:

Week 10: Chapters 8 – 14

1. What does the fool say from his heart? Contrast that with the comments and thoughts from the wise.

___

___

___

2. Why is a man blessed who "does not stand in the way of sinners"? What was Jesus' example of this posture?

___

___

___

3. Where does David take refuge? Did he love Saul and revere his kingdom? What were the results?

___

___

___

* Space is provided for additional notations at the end of the course.

Course III, *Book of Psalms**
Suggested Reading Schedule and Discussion:

Week 11: Chapters 15 – 16, 22, 35, 41, 68-69

1. What things can a man do and never be shaken? Is this true for all mankind or only the ancient Psalmist?

___

___

___

2. Psalm 35 is the "fight song". How so? What are the different moods or conditions portrayed by Psalms?

___

___

___

3. What are the attributes of the Lord for David in Psalm 41? Who wrote the majority of the prophetic Psalms?

___

___

___

* Space is provided for additional notations at the end of the course.

Course III, *Book of Psalms**
Suggested Reading Schedule and Discussion:

Week 12: Chapters 70 – 72, 118, 132

1. What was David's petition in Psalm 70? What was the reason and what were the results?

____

____

____

2. Why should we give thanks to the Lord? Should this be a continual activity and how do we give thanks?

____

____

____

3. What was the Lord's oath to David? Can you think of other oaths in the Bible given by the Lord? To whom?

____

____

____

* Space is provided for additional notations at the end of the course.

- *"The LORD is my shepherd, I shall not be in want. He makes me lie down in green pastures, he leads me beside quiet waters, he restores my soul. He guides me in paths of righteousness for his name's sake. Even though I walk through the valley of the shadow of death, I will fear no evil, for you are with me; your rod and your staff, they comfort me. You prepare a table before me in the presence of my enemies. You anoint my head with oil; my cup overflows. Surely goodness and love will follow me all the days of my life, and I will dwell in the house of the LORD forever. (Psalms 23:1-6)*

- *"Ascribe to the LORD, O mighty ones, ascribe to the LORD glory and strength. ...worship the LORD in the splendor of his holiness." (Psalm 29:1-2)*

- *"Blessed are they whose ways are blameless, who walk according to the law of the LORD. Blessed are they who keep his statutes and seek him with all their heart." Psalm 119:1-2*[71]

[71] http://www.gotquestions.org/Book-of-Psalms.html

The End of Course Three

(Please jot down any additional notations which may be helpful in group discussions.)

VII. WISDOM SERIES

The books of Job, Proverbs and Ecclesiastes.

Job is the oldest book in the Bible. It records the plight of righteous Job, his many detractors, and his victory in the end. Proverbs is a collection of Jewish phrases, sayings and prophesies, most of which are true to this day. Ecclesiastes gives an honest and reasonable account of King Solomon's "reasoning under the Sun".

Course One:	**The Book of Job**
Course Two:	**The Book of Proverbs**
Course Three:	**The Book of Ecclesiastes**

Series VII. Course I
Book of Job

Most scholars suggest authorship as either Job, Elihu, Moses or Solomon. The **Book of Job** (Hebrew: אִיּוֹב) is one of the books of the Hebrew Bible. It relates the story of Job, his trials at the hands of the Satan, his theological discussions with friends on the origins and nature of his suffering, his challenge to God, and finally a response from God.

The Book itself, along with its numerous exegeses, are attempts to address the problem of evil, (i.e. the problem of reconciling the existence of evil or suffering in the world with the existence of God).

A great diversity of opinion exists as to the origin of this book and the identity of Job. The book of Job begins, “There was a man in the land of Uz, whose name was Job.” The Epistle of James declares, “Ye have heard of the patience of Job” (Jas. 5.11), whilst Ezekiel, speaking of judgment to come upon the land, says, “Though these three men, Noah, Daniel and Job, were in it, they should deliver but their own souls” (Ezek. 14.14).

The Talmud (***Tractate Bava Basra 15a-b***) maintains that the Book of Job was written by Moses, although the Sages dispute whether it was based on historical reality or intended as a parable. Although Moses' authorship is accepted as definitive, other opinions in the Talmud ascribe it to the period of before the First Temple, the time of the patriarch Jacob, or King Ahaserud.

Comparative literary and historical examinations of the text more generally conclude that, though archaic features such as the "council in heaven" survive, and though the story of Job was familiar to Ezekiel (Chapter 14 verse 14), the present form of Job was fixed in the postexilic period 6th century BC - 5th century BC.

Job was very prosperous, and had seven sons and three daughters. Constantly fearing that his sons may have sinned and "cursed God in their hearts", he habitually offered burnt offerings as a pardon for their sins. The "sons of God" and Satan (literally, the Hebrew word means "the accuser" or "the adversary") present themselves to God.

God asks Satan his opinion on Job, apparently a truly pious man. Satan answers that Job is pious only because he is prosperous. In response to Satan's assertion, God gives Satan permission to destroy Job's possessions and family.

All of Job's possessions are destroyed and a '**ruach**' (wind/spirit) causes the house of the firstborn to collapse killing all of Job's offspring who were gathered for a feast. Job does not curse God after this but instead shaves his head, tears his clothes and says, "Naked I came out of my mother's womb, and naked shall I return : YHVH has given, and YHVH has taken away; blessed be the name of YHVH". So despite all Job's sufferings, his response is to worship the Lord.

As Job was pondering the cause of his misery, three questions came to his mind, all of which are answered only in our Lord Jesus Christ. These questions occur in chapter 14. First, in verse 4, Job asks, "Who can bring what is pure from the impure? No one!?" Job's question comes from a heart that recognizes it cannot possibly please God or become justified in His sight. God is holy; we are not. Therefore, a great gulf exists between man and God, caused by sin. But the answer to Job's anguished question is found in Jesus Christ. He has paid the penalty for our sin and has exchanged it for His righteousness, thereby making us acceptable in God's sight (Hebrews 10:14; Colossians 1:21-23; 2 Corinthians 5:17).

Summary Information:[72]

Book of Job	
Chapters:	**42**
Verses:	**1070**
Verses of Prophecy (Fulfilled):	**1**
Verses of Prophecy (Unfulfilled):	**3**

[72] http://en.wikipedia.org/wiki/Book_of_Job

Course I, *Book of Job**
Suggested Reading Schedule and Discussion:

Week 1: Chapters 1 – 2, 15 - 19

1. Why was Job the greatest man of the people of the East? What was his attitude toward God?

___

___

___

2. What agreement did God have with Satan regarding Job? What prompted this discussion regarding Job?

___

___

___

3. How did Job respond to Eliphaz and Bildad? Were these men lifelong friends of Job that he trusted?

___

___

___

* Space is provided for additional notations at the end of the course.

Course I, *Book of Job**
Suggested Reading Schedule and Discussion:

Week 2: Chapters 20 – 26

1. How did Job reply to Zophar the Naamathite? Why did Job disagree with Zophar and what were the results?

___

___

___

2. Does the almighty set times for immediate or delayed judgment? Why is time perceived differently by God?

___

___

___

3. Why do we have difficulty understanding God's power or judgment? What can we do to more fully understand Him?

___

___

___

* Space is provided for additional notations at the end of the course.

Course I, *Book of Job**
Suggested Reading Schedule and Discussion:

Week 3: Chapters 27 – 33

1. Did Job really believe that God had denied him justice? Was his wife supportive in his decision?

____

____

____

2. Did Job believe that God continually watched over him? How and when did Job communicate with God?

____

____

____

3. Why did the three men stop answering Job? Were these men ultimately Job's true and tested friends?

____

____

____

* Space is provided for additional notations at the end of the course.

Course I, *Book of Job**
Suggested Reading Schedule and Discussion:

Week 4: Chapters 34 – 38, 42

1. What was Elihu's final position? How would we have judged Job's position if we had witnessed everything that happened to Job as Elihu did? Was he wrong?

___

___

___

2. Did Job believe that God had no regard for the wise in heart? What was his final inheritance before God?

___

___

___

3. Why was the Lord angry with Eliphaz, Bildad and Zophar? What was his action toward Job's wife?

___

___

___

* Space is provided for additional notations at the end of the course.

- *"In the land of Uz there lived a man whose name was Job. This man was blameless and upright; he feared God and shunned evil. He had seven sons and three daughters, and he owned seven thousand sheep, three thousand camels, five hundred yoke of oxen and five hundred donkeys, and had a large number of servants. He was the greatest man among all the people of the East." (Job 1:1-3)*

- *Naked I came from my mother's womb, and naked I will depart. The LORD gave and the LORD has taken away; may the name of the LORD be praised." (Job 1:21)*

- *The LORD blessed the latter part of Job's life more than the first. He had fourteen thousand sheep, six thousand camels,... And he also had seven sons and three daughters. ...After this, Job lived a hundred and forty years; he saw his children and their children to the fourth generation. And so he died, old and full of years. (Job 42: 12-17)*[73]

[73] http://www.gotquestions.org/Book-of-Job.html

The End of Course One

(Please jot down any additional notations which may be helpful in group discussions.)

Series VII. Course II
Book of Proverbs

King Solomon is the principal writer of Proverbs. His name appears in 1:1, 10:1, and 25:1. We may also presume Solomon collected and edited proverbs other than his own, for Ecclesiastes 12:9 says, "Not only was the Teacher wise, but also he imparted knowledge to the people. He pondered and searched out and set in order many proverbs."

The Book of Proverbs (in Hebrew: מִשְׁלֵי *Mishley*) is a book of the Hebrew Bible (the Christian Old Testament), included in the collected works known as the "Writings" or Ketuvim.

In 1 Kings 4:29-34, 3000 proverbs and over 1000 songs are said to have come from Solomon and it is also said that people came from all over to hear the wisdom of Solomon.

The book of Proverbs is referred to as wisdom literature along with several others: the book of Job, Ecclesiastes, the Song of Solomon, and certain Psalms, known as wisdom psalms. Among the deuterocanonical books, Ecclesiasticus and the Wisdom of Solomon are wisdom literature.

The general assumption is that Solomon was a part of the authorship to some extent, but that the book was not solely his work. Not only are the names "Agur" and "Lemuel" linked to other sections of the book, there are elements of disunity within the book that suggest more than one author. Some of the authorship is attributed to "Men of Hezekiah" (25:1), though it is stated that they simply transcribed the proverbs rather than writing them of their own accord.

Solomon's proverbs were penned around 900 B.C. During his reign as king, the nation of Israel reached its pinnacle spiritually, politically, culturally, and economically.

As Israel's reputation soared, so did King Solomon's. Foreign dignitaries from the far reaches of the known world traveled great distances to hear the wise monarch speak (1 Kings 4:34)Throughout Proverbs, wisdom (or the wise person) is compared and contrasted with foolishness (or the fool). 'Fool' in Proverbs indicates one who is lacking in morality and uninterested in correction, not one who is merely silly or playful. Wisdom is held up as something worth effort to attain and the reader is told that it starts with the person of Yahweh:

"The fear of Yahweh is the beginning of wisdom". The theme of wisdom finds its fulfillment in Christ. We are continually exhorted in Proverbs to seek wisdom, get wisdom, and understand wisdom. Proverbs also tells us—and repeats it— that the fear of the Lord is the beginning of wisdom (1:7; 9:10). The wisdom that is found only in Christ is in contrast to the foolishness of the world which encourages us to be wise in our own eyes. But Proverbs also tells us that the world's way is not God's way (Proverbs 3:7) and leads only to death.

Summarizing the Book of Proverbs is a bit difficult, for unlike many other books of Scripture, there is no particular plot or storyline found in its pages; likewise, there are no principal characters in the book. It is wisdom that takes center stage—a grand, divine wisdom that transcends the whole of history, peoples, and cultures. Even a perfunctory reading of this magnificent treasury reveals the pithy sayings of the wise King Solomon are as relevant today as they were then. .

Summary Information:[74]

Book of Proverbs	
Chapters:	**31**
Verses:	**915**
Verses of Prophecy (Fulfilled):	**0**
Verses of Prophecy (Unfulfilled):	**27**

[74] ttp://en.wikipedia.org/wiki/Book_of_Proverbs

Course II, *Book of Proverbs**
Suggested Reading Schedule and Discussion:

Week 5: Chapters 1 – 7

1. Who wrote the book of Proverbs? Was it intended to be a compilation of Jewish wisdom? What period?

___

___

___

2. What are the purpose and theme of Proverbs? Are the sayings as true today as when they were written?

___

___

___

3. What are the general benefits of Wisdom? Why does the writer focus on wisdom as a key virtue?

___

___

___

* Space is provided for additional notations at the end of the course.

Course II, *Book of Proverbs**
Suggested Reading Schedule and Discussion:

Week 6: Chapters 8 – 14

1. What is the opposite of Wisdom? Why is the opposite so despicable to the Lord and wisdom so revered?

____

____

____

2. What are the warnings against the adulteress? What were the results of adultery in ancient Israel and today?

____

____

____

3. Discuss some of the more interesting proverbs. Relate them to our culture and society today.

____

____

____

* Space is provided for additional notations at the end of the course.

Course II, *Book of Proverbs**
Suggested Reading Schedule and Discussion:

Week 7: Chapters 15 – 21

1. What happens when one has pride? Why is pride one of the foremost sins against God?

____

____

____

2. What does Proverbs generally say about the mouth, tongue and speech? How does the Bible suggest that we communicate?

____

____

____

3. More general proverbs. Good discussion points? Find proverbs about money or the accumulation of wealth.

____

____

* Space is provided for additional notations at the end of the course.

Course II, *Book of Proverbs**
Suggested Reading Schedule and Discussion:

Week 8: Chapters 29 – 31

1. How does Solomon view a quarrelsome wife? What was his marital status in the palace?

____

____

____

2. Discuss the sayings of Agur. Who was this wise person and what relation did he have with Solomon?

____

____

____

3. Discuss the sayings of King Lemuel. Again Who was this wise person and what relation did he have with Solomon?

____

____

____

* Space is provided for additional notations at the end of the course.

- *"The fear of the LORD is the beginning of knowledge, but fools despise wisdom and discipline."* (Proverbs 1:7)

- *"Get wisdom, get understanding; do not forget my words or swerve from them."* (Proverbs 4:5)

- *"To fear the LORD is to hate evil; I hate pride and arrogance, evil behavior and perverse speech. Counsel and sound judgment are mine; I have understanding and power.'"* (Proverbs 8:13-14)

- *Better to live on a corner of the roof than share a house with a quarrelsome wife.* (Proverbs 21:9)

- *Discipline your son, and he will give you peace; he will bring delight to your soul.* (Proverbs 29:17)[75]

[75] http://www.gotquestions.org/Book-of-Proverbs.html

The End of Course Two

(Please jot down any additional notations which may be helpful in group discussions.)

Series VII. Course III
Book of Ecclesiastes

The Book of Ecclesiastes does not directly identify its author. There are quite a few verses that imply Solomon wrote this book. There are some clues in the context that may suggest a different person wrote the book after Solomon's death, possibly several hundred years later. The belief is that the author is indeed Solomon.

Ecclesiastes (often abbreviated *Ecc*) (Hebrew: קֹהֶלֶת, *Kohelet*, variously transliterated as *Kohelet*, *Qoheleth*, *Koheles*, *Koheleth*, or *Coheleth*) is a book of the Hebrew Bible. The English name derives from the Greek translation of the Hebrew title.

According to Talmud, however, the point of Qohelet is to state that all is futile under the Sun. One should therefore ignore physical pleasures and put all one's efforts towards that which is *above* the Sun. This is summed up in the second to last verse: "The end of the matter; all has been heard. Fear God, and keep his commandments; for that is the whole duty of everyone" (12:13)

The main speaker in the book, identified by the name or title Qohelet, introduces himself as "son of David, and king in Jerusalem. "The work emphatically proclaims all the actions of man to be inherently "vain", "futile", "empty", "meaningless", "temporary", "transitory", or "fleeting," depending on translation, as the lives of both wise and foolish men end in death.

Ecclesiastes is a book of perspective. The narrative of "the Preacher" (KJV), or "the Teacher" (NIV) reveals the depression that results from seeking happiness in worldly things. It gives Christians a chance to see the world through the eyes of a person who, though wise, is trying to find meaning in temporary, human things

.

Two phrases are repeated often in Ecclesiastes. The word translated as "vanity" in the KJV, and "meaningless" in the NIV appears often, and is used to emphasize the temporary nature of worldly things. In the end, even the most impressive human achievements will be left behind. The phrase "under the sun" occurs 28 times, and refers to the mortal world. When the Preacher refers to "all things under the sun," he is talking about earthly, temporary, human things.

The first seven chapters of the book of Ecclesiastes describe all of the worldly things "under the sun" that the Preacher tries to find fulfillment in. He tries scientific discovery (1:10-11), wisdom and philosophy (1:13-18), mirth (2:1), alcohol (2:3), architecture (2:4), property (2:7-8), and luxury (2:8). He found that everything was meaningless, a temporary diversion that, without God, had no purpose or longevity.

Chapters 8-12 of Ecclesiastes describe the Preacher's suggestions and comments on how a life should be lived. He comes to the conclusion that without God, there is no truth or meaning to life. So he advises to acknowledge God from youth (12:1) and to follow His will (12:13-14).

In the end, the Preacher comes to accept that faith in God is the only way to find personal meaning. He decides to accept the fact that life is brief and ultimately worthless without God. The Preacher advises the reader to focus on an eternal God instead of temporary pleasure.

For all of the vanities described in the Book of Ecclesiastes, the answer is Christ. According to Ecclesiastes 3:17, God judges the righteous and the wicked, and the righteous are only those who are in Christ (2 Corinthians 5:21). God has placed the desire for eternity in our hearts

(Ecclesiastes 3:11) and has provided the Way to eternal life through Christ (John 3:16).

Summary Information[76]:

Book of Ecclesiastes	
Chapters:	12
Verses:	222
Verses of Prophecy (Fulfilled):	0
Verses of Prophecy (Unfulfilled):	0

[76] ttp://en.wikipedia.org/wiki/Book_of_Ecclesiastes

Course III, *Book of Ecclesiastes**
Suggested Reading Schedule and Discussion:

Week 9: Chapters 1 – 7

1. Who wrote Ecclesiastes and for what purpose? Can this book be construed as the more sarcastic in the bible? What is the sarcasm?

___

___

___

2. Why is everything meaningless according to the teacher? Who was the teacher and why was he qualified?

___

___

___

3. Discuss the famous "A time for everything". This is a true litany of life to end the bible study series. Ponder,

___

___

___

* Space is provided for additional notations at the end of the course.

Course III, *Book of Ecclesiastes**
Suggested Reading Schedule and Discussion:

Week 10: Chapters 8 – 12

1. What is a common destiny for all? To whom do we owe our being and everything that we are?

____

____

____

2. What happens when you "cast your bread upon the waters"? What did Jesus say about this prophecy?

____

____

____

3. What is the conclusion of the matter? (*I'll answer this one for you*), Our life is only meaningful in the context of God the Father, God the Son, and God the Holy Spirit...in whom we live and have our being. Shalom.

____

____

____

* Space is provided for additional notations at the end of the course.

- *Remember your Creator in the days of your youth, before the days of trouble come and the years approach when you will say, "I find no pleasure in them" (Ecclesiastes 1:1)*

- *"Vanity of vanities, says the Preacher, vanity of vanities, all is vanity" (NKJV). (Ecclesiastes 1:2)*

- *"For with much wisdom comes much sorrow; the more knowledge, the more grief." (Ecclesiastes 1:18)*

- *"Yet when I surveyed all that my hands had done and what I had toiled to achieve, everything was meaningless, a chasing after the wind; nothing was gained under the sun." (Ecclesiastes 2:11)*

- *"Now all has been heard; here is the conclusion... Fear God and keep his commandments, for this is the whole duty of man. For God will bring every deed into judgment, including every hidden thing, whether it is good or evil." (Ecclesiastes 12:13)*[77]

[77] http://www.gotquestions.org/Book-of-Ecclesiastes.html

The End of Course Three

(Please jot down any additional notations which may be helpful in group discussions.)

THE LENTEN SERIES

The popular 5-part Lenten series compares the Major Religions of the World.

The Abrahamic religions of Judaism, Islam and Christianity are compared as well as prominent Eastern Religions. Finally, a summary indicates high-level world percentages and summary information of each major religion.

Week One:	**Jesus the Christ and His chosen Apostles**
Week Two:	**Why Judaism will not accept Christianity**
Week Three:	**Understanding Islam**
Week Four:	**Eastern Religions**
Week Five:	**Summary: Major Religions of the World**

THE LENTEN SERIES

Week 1

JESUS THE CHRIST

AND HIS CHOSEN APOSTLES

Christ[78]

An English term for the Greek **Χριστός (*Khristós*)** meaning "the anointed one". It is a translation of the Hebrew **מָשִׁיחַ (*Māšîaḥ*).** The word is often misunderstood to be the surname of Jesus due to the numerous mentions of *Jesus Christ* in the Christian Bible. The word is in fact used as a title, hence its common reciprocal use *Christ Jesus*, meaning ***The Anointed One,*** *Jesus*. Followers of Jesus became known as Christians because they believed that Jesus was the Christ, or Messiah, prophesied about in the Tanakh (which Christians term the Old Testament). The majority of Jews reject this claim and are still waiting for Christ to come. Most Christians now wait for the Second Coming of Christ when they believe he will fulfill the rest of the Messianic prophecy. In the Septuagint version of the Hebrew Bible, it was used to translate into Greek the Hebrew ***mashiach* (messiah)**, meaning "anointed." *Khristós* in classical Greek usage could mean *covered in oil,* and is thus a literal translation of messiah. The New Testament records that the Messiah, long awaited, had come and describes this savior as *The Christ.* The famous Jewish historian, Flavius Josephus, wrote in his ***Antiquities of the Jews (93-94 AD):***

[78] www.en.wikipedia.org/wiki/Jesus_Christ
www.gotquestions.org/Jesus-Christ.htm

"Now there was about this time Jesus, a wise man, if it be lawful to call him a man; for he was a doer of wonderful works, a teacher of such men as receive the truth with pleasure. He drew over to him both many of the Jews and many of the Gentiles. He was Christ. And when Pilate, at the suggestion of the principal men amongst us, had condemned him to the cross, those that loved him at the first did not forsake him; for he appeared to them alive again the third day, as the divine prophets had foretold these and ten thousand other wonderful things concerning him. And the tribe of Christians, so named from him, are not extinct at this day."

The word Apostle, (Ancient Greek: **ἀπόστολος** *apostolos)*, is defined as one sent forth as a messenger. They were, according to the Acts of the Apostles and Christian tradition, *disciples* whom Jesus of Nazareth had chosen, named, and trained in order to send them on a specific mission: the establishment of the Christian church by evangelism and the spreading of the "good news", after being sent the Holy Spirit as "helper" (paraclete) in this task at Pentecost.

"From Jerusalem there went out twelve men into the world. These men were uneducated and of no ability in speaking. But by the power of God, they proclaimed to every race of men that they were sent by Christ to teach the word of God to everyone"-Justin Martyr, (c. 160 *AD*)

According to Clement of Alexandria, St. Peter and St. Philip were married and had children, and St. Paul probably did, too. Their wives traveled with the Apostles "not as wives, but as sisters, in order to minister to housewives". Clement also reports that St. Peter's wife was martyred before him, and the apostle encouraged her as she was led to her death. St. Peter and St. Paul founded the church in Rome and were martyred there under Nero.. St. John is traditionally thought to have been exiled to the island of Patmos, where he wrote the apocalyptic Book of Revelation. This is stated in Revelation itself (1:9) and confirmed by Clement of Alexandria and Tertullian., The initial twelve apostles were named in all three of the Synoptic Gospels.

(***Matthew 10:1-4; Mark 3:15-18, and Luke 6:12-15*). St. Paul, the "least Apostle" to be chosen by Jesus Christ, was recorded in the ***Acts of the Apostles***:

> **He called his twelve disciples to him and gave them authority to drive out evil spirits and to heal every disease and sickness. These are the names of the twelve apostles: first, Simon (who is called Peter) and his brother Andrew; James son of Zebedee, and his brother John; Philip and Bartholomew; Thomas and Matthew the tax collector; James son of Alphaeus, and Thaddeus; [4]Simon the Zealot and Judas Iscariot, who betrayed him. (*Matthew 10:1-4*)**

> **As he neared Damascus on his journey, suddenly a light from heaven flashed around him. He fell to the ground and heard a voice say to him, "Saul, Saul, why do you persecute me?" "Who are you, Lord?" Saul asked. "I am Jesus, whom you are persecuting," he replied. "Now get up and go into the city, and you will be told what you must do... But the Lord said to Ananias, "Go! This man is my chosen instrument to carry my name before the Gentiles and their kings and before the people of Israel. I will show him how much he must suffer for my name." *(Acts 9:3-6, 15-16)***

St. Peter[79]

Simon Peter Greek: **Πέτρος**, *Pétros* "Rock", *Kephas* in Hellenized Aramaic) (c.1–64 *AD*) was a leader of the early Christian Church, who features prominently in the New Testament Gospels and the Acts of the Apostles. Peter was the son of John, and was from the village of Bethsaida in the province of Galilee. His brother Andrew was also an apostle. In a famous passage, Jesus addressed His Apostles, "But whom do you say that I am?" Simon (St. Peter) said: "Thou art Christ,

[79] www.en.wikipedia.org/wiki/St. Peter
www.gotquestions.org/Apostles.htm

the Son of the living God". And Jesus answering said to him: "Blessed art thou, Simon Bar-Jona: because flesh and blood hath not revealed it to thee, but my Father who is in heaven. And I say to thee: That thou art Peter [***Kipha,*** a rock], and upon this rock, I will build my church and the gates of hell shall not prevail against it. And I will give to thee the keys of the kingdom of heaven. And whatsoever thou shalt bind upon earth, it shall be bound also in heaven: and whatsoever thou shalt loose on earth, it shall be loosed also in heaven" (***Matthew 16:13-20; Mark 8:27-30; Luke 9:18-21).***

During Christ's passion at the cross, St. .Peter at first took to flight with the other Apostles ***(John 18:10-11; Matthew 26:56)***; then turning he followed his captured Lord to the courtyard of the High Priest, and there denied Christ, asserting explicitly and swearing that he knew Him not (***Matthew 26:58-75; Mark 14:54-72; Luke 22:54-62; John 18:15-27***). Later, it is recorded after His resurrection, Christ appeared at the Lake of Genesareth and renewed to Peter His special commission to feed and defend His flock. (***John 21:15-17)***. St. Peter traveled widely preaching the Gospel. After having been the Bishop of Antioch and having preached to the ones who were scattered (i.e. (Hebrews and Hebrew Christians), in Pontus, Galatia, Cappadocia, Asia and Bithynia, St. Peter went to Rome. In the second year of Claudius he overthrew Simon Magus, and held the Sacerdotal Chair for 25 years. St. Peter worked among the Jews before he eventually reached Rome, where he was traditionally the first bishop. ***Mark's Gospel*** is based on St. Peter's teaching, and St. Peter wrote ***The First Letter of St. Peter.*** Apocryphal works associated with his name, but dating from the 2nd century and later include the ***Gospel of St. Peter*** and the ***Apocalypse or Revelation of St. Peter.***

Catholic tradition states the St Peter was the "Prince of Apostles", the first Pope and founder of the see of Rome. In the early fourth century, the Emperor Constantine I decided to honor St. Peter with a large basilica. However, the protestant view remains that "We honor St. Peter and in fact some of our churches are named after him, but he was not the first pope, nor was he Roman Catholic.

Along with the Apostle Paul, he may have been executed around 64 AD during the persecutions of Emperor Nero, or later in 67-68 AD. Apparently he was crucified, head-down, at his own request. His relics are believed to be housed beneath St. Peter's Basilica in the Vatican.

St. James, Son of Zebedee[80]

St. James, son of Zebedee (d. 44 *AD*) or **Yaakov Ben-Zebdi/Bar-Zebdi**, was one of the Twelve Apostles of Jesus. He was a son of Zebedee and Salome, and brother of John the Apostle. He is also called ***James the Greater*** to distinguish him from St. James, son of Alphaeus, also known as James the Less. The Synoptic Gospels state that James and John were with their father by the seashore when Jesus called them to follow him. Before his death, St. James preached in Jerusalem and Judea.

Acts 12:1-2 - "It was at this time (of great famine, possibly around 44 AD), that King Herod laid violent hands on some of the Church members. St. James, St. John's brother, he executed with the sword (beheaded) ....." According to the tradition, he had not yet left Jerusalem at this time.

St. John[81]

John the Apostle (Greek **Ιωάννης**) (c. 6 - c. 100 *AD*) was one of the Twelve Apostles of Jesus. He was the son of Zebedee

[80] www.en.wikipedia.org/wiki/St. James
[81] www.en.wikipedia.org/wiki/St. John

and Salome, and brother of James, another of the Twelve Apostles. Saint John the Apostle was the son of Zebedee, and the brother of Saint James the Greater. The Eastern Orthodox tradition gives his mother's name as Salome. They originally were fishermen and fished with their father in the Lake of Genesareth. He was first a disciple of St. John the Baptist and later one of the twelve apostles of Jesus. When St. John was aged, he trained Polycarp who later became Bishop of Smyrna. This was important because Polycarp was able to carry John's message to future generations (He taught Irenaeus).

Roman Catholic tradition states that St. John and the Virgin Mary moved to Ephesus, where they eventually died, though there is an alternative tradition that holds Mary's death to be in Jerusalem, where her tomb is, a tradition held true by Orthodox Christians. Some believe, however, that there is support for the idea that ‘St. John did go to Ephesus and from there wrote the three epistles traditionally attributed to him. St. John was allegedly banished by the Roman authorities to the Greek island of Patmos, where some believe that he wrote the ***Book of Revelation***. Christian tradition identifies him as the author of several New Testament works: the ***Gospel of John***, the ***Epistles of John***, and the ***Book of Revelation***.

According to ***St. John's Gospel (19:26-27***), it was probably “St. John who took Mary, the mother of Jesus as his adopted mother. He preached in Jerusalem, and later, as bishop of Ephesus, south of Izmir in western Turkey, worked among the churches of Asia Minor during the reigns of either Emperor Nero (54-68 *AD*) or Domitian (81-96 *AD*).

Tertullian added that St. John was thrust into boiling oil in Rome without being hurt before he was sent into exile. Irenaeus, writing earlier (c. 180 *AD*), speaks only of John's career with the church in Ephesus, where he "remained among them permanently until the time of Trajan". Polycrates reports that John was a martyr and was buried at Ephesus. Clement of Alexandria explains that St. John returned to Ephesus from

Patmos upon "the tyrant's death" and a century later Victorinus elaborates that Domitian had condemned St. John to Patmos to work the mines, but when the Caesar died, St. John was released and returned to Ephesus, where he wrote his Gospel.

St. John was banished to the island of Patmos, now one of the Greek islands in the Aegean Sea. He was subsequently freed and died a natural death, possibly the only Apostle of the "original twelve" to do so, at Ephesus c 100 AD.

St. Philip[82]

St Philip was one of the twelve Apostles of Jesus. Later Christian traditions describe St. Philip as the apostle who preached in Greece, Syria, and Phrygia. The ***Gospel of John*** describes St. Philip's calling as a disciple of Jesus ***(John 1:43).*** St. Philip is described as a disciple from the city of Bethsaida, and connects him to St. Andrew and St. Peter, who were from the same town (***John 1:43–44)***. It further connects him to Nathanael (sometimes identified with St. Bartholomew), by describing how St. Philip introduced Nathaniel to Jesus ***(John 1:45–47***). The authors of the Synoptic Gospels also describe St. Philip as a disciple of Jesus. The "Apostle should be distinguished from Philip the "deacon" or Evangelist, who preached to the people of Samaria and baptized the Ethiopian eunuch,(***Acts 8:4-8,26-39.)***

St. Philip preached the Gospel in Phrygia (west central Turkey) before dying or being martyred there at Hieropolis. He was martyred by crucifixion. Included in the Acts of Philip is an appendix, entitled "Of the Journeyings of Philip the Apostle: From the Fifteenth Act Until the End, and Among Them the Martyrdom." This appendix gives an account of 'St. Philip's martyrdom in the city of Hierapolis.

82 www.en.wikipedia.org/wiki/St. Philip

St. Bartholomew[83]

St. Bartholomew was one of the twelve Apostles of Jesus. *Bartholomew* (Greek: **Βαρθολομαίος,** transliterated "Bartholomaios") comes from the Aramaic *bar-Tôlmay* (**תולמי-בר**), meaning *son of Tolmay* (Ptolemy) or *son of the furrows* (perhaps a ploughman). Though St. Bartholomew was listed among the Twelve Apostles in the three **Synoptic gospels*: Matthew, Mark, and Luke,*** and also appears as one of the witnesses of the Ascension, each time named in the company of St. Philip, he is one of the apostles of whom no word is reported nor any individual action recorded in the New Testament. ***Eusebius of Caesarea*'s Ecclesiastical History (v §10)** states that after the Ascension, Bartholomew went on a missionary tour to India, where he left behind a copy of the Gospel of St. Matthew. Along with his fellow Apostle St. Jude, St. Bartholomew is reputed to have brought Christianity to Armenia in the 1st century.

The missionary work of St. Bartholomew is linked with Armenia (present day Armenia, eastern Turkey, northern Iraq, north western Iran) and India. Other locations include Egypt, Arabia, Ethiopia and Persia (Iran).

Traditionally, St. Bartholomew met his death by being flayed or skinned alive, and then beheaded. Derbent, north of present day Baku on the Caspian Sea, may have been his place of martyrdom. Alternatively he may have suffered this cruel fate in what is now India.

St. Thomas[84]

St. Thomas the Apostle, also called **Doubting Thomas** or **Didymus** (meaning "Twin"), was one of the Twelve Apostles of Jesus. He is best known for disbelieving Jesus' resurrection

83 www.en.wikipedia.org/wiki/St. Bartholomew
84 www.en.wikipedia.org/wiki/St. Thomas

when first told of it, then proclaiming "My Lord and my God" on seeing Jesus in ***John 20:28***. He was perhaps the only Apostle who went outside the Roman Empire to preach the Gospel. He also crossed the largest area, which includes the Persian Empire and India. Syrian tradition also states that the apostle's full name was Judas Thomas, or Jude Thomas.

Just as the Apostles St. Peter and St. Paul are said to have brought the fledgling Christianity to Greece and Rome, Saint Mark brought it to Egypt, Saint John to Syria and Asia Minor, St. Thomas is often said to have taken it eastwards as far as India. St. Thomas may have labored for the Gospel in Parthia (including modern Iraq and Iran), but stronger traditions link him with southern India. Mount St. Thomas, close to Madras, is associated with his Apocryphal writings which include the 3rd or 4th century ***Acts of Thomas***, and the ***Gospel of Thomas.***

Indian Christians from the west coast Kerala area claim they were evangelized by St. Thomas, who was later speared to death near Madras on the east coast. He was a martyr and was killed by group of sages in Chennai and the Place is called Saint Thomas Mount.

St. Matthew[85]

St. Matthew the Evangelist (**מתי/מתתיהו,** "Gift of Yahweh", Standard Hebrew and Tiberian Hebrew: *Mattay* or *Mattithyahu*; Septuagint Greek: **Ματθαίος,** *Matthaios*, Modern Greek: **Ματθαίος**, *Matthaíos*), most often called Saint Matthew, is a Christian figure, and one of Jesus's Twelve Apostles. He is credited by tradition with writing the ***Gospel of Matthew,*** and is identified in that gospel as being the same person as Levi the publican (tax-collector). Nothing definite is known of St. Matthew's career.

85 www.en.wikipedia.org/wiki/St. Matthew

After preaching in Judea, different traditions place St. Matthew's missionary work and possible martyrdom in Ethiopia or Persia.

St. James, Son of Alphaeus[86]

Saint James, son of Alphaeus (Ἰάκωβος, *Jacobos* in Greek) was one of the Twelve Apostles of Jesus Christ. St. James, son of Alphaeus, only appears four times in the New Testament, each time in a list of the twelve apostles. Known as James the Less, to distinguish him from James the Greater, son of Zebedee, but more likely because of his smaller stature than his relative importance. He, and Jude following, should not be confused with James and Jude (or Judas), the brothers of Jesus. Most commentators treat them as separate sets of brothers.

Tradition claims he first worked in Palestine (Israel) before preaching and martyrdom in Egypt. He is reported to have been martyred by crucifixion at Ostrakine in Lower Egypt, where he was preaching the Gospel. A carpenter's saw is the symbol associated with him in Christian art because it is also noted that his body was later sawed to pieces.

St. Jude[87]

St. Jude was one of the Twelve Apostles of Jesus. He is generally identified with **Thaddeus**, and is also variously called **Jude of James**, **Jude Thaddaeus**, **Judas Thaddaeus** or **Lebbaeus**. He is sometimes identified with Jude, brother of

86 www.en.wikipedia.org/wiki/St. James, son of Alphaeus
87 www.en.wikipedia.org/wiki/St. Jude

Jesus, but is clearly distinguished from Judas Iscariot, another disciple and later the betrayer of Jesus. Opinion is divided on whether St. Jude the Apostle is the same as Jude, brother of Jesus, who is mentioned in ***Mark 6:3*** and ***Matthew 13:55-57***, and is the traditional author of the ***Epistle of St. Jude.*** Tradition holds that Saint Jude preached the Gospel in Judea, Samaria, Idumaea, Syria, Mesopotamia and Libya. He is also said to have visited Beirut and Edessa, though the emissary of latter mission is also identified as Thaddeus of Edessa, one of 70.

St. Jude may have preached in Assyria (eastern Iraq) and Persia (Iran), before joining with Simon the Zealot and being killed with him in Persia.

St. Simon[88]

The Apostle is called **St. Simon Zelotes**, **Simon the Zealot**, in Luke 6:15 and Acts 1:13; and **Simon Kananaios** or **Simon Cananeus** ("Simon" signifying **שמעון** "hearkening; listening", Standard Hebrew **Šimon**, Tiberian Hebrew **Šimôn**), was one of the most obscure among the Apostles of Jesus. To distinguish him from St.(Simon) Peter, he is called *Kananaios*, or *Kananites* (***Matthew 10:4; Mark 3:18)***, and in the list of Apostles in ***Luke 6:15***, and repeated in ***Acts 1:13***. The most widespread tradition is that after evangelizing in Egypt, St. Simon joined St. Jude in Persia and Armenia, where both were martyred. One tradition states that he travelled in the Middle East and Africa. St. Simon is referred to both as the "Cananaean" and the "Zealot".

The tradition is that St. Simon first preached in Egypt, before joining St. Jude and traveling to Persia, where both were martyred. St. Simon may have been crucified or hacked to death.

---

[88] www.en.wikipedia.org/wiki/St. Simon

Judas Iscariot[89]

Judas Iscariot, Hebrew: **יהודה איש־קריות "Yehuda" Yəhûḏāh Îš-qəriyyôṯ** was, according to the New Testament, one of the twelve original Apostles of Jesus. Among the twelve, he was apparently designated to keep account of the "money bag" (Grk. **γλωσσόκομον)**, but he is most traditionally known for his role in Jesus' betrayal into the hands of Roman authorities.

According to the account given in the Gospel of John, Judas carried the disciples' money bag and betrayed Jesus for a bribe of "thirty pieces of silver" by identifying him with a kiss—"the kiss of Judas"—to arresting soldiers of the High Priest Caiaphas, who then turned Jesus over to Pontius Pilate's soldiers.

The ***Gospel of Matthew*** says that, after Jesus' arrest by the Roman authorities (but before his execution), the guilt-ridden Judas returned the bribe to the priests and committed suicide by hanging. The priests, forbidden by Jewish law from returning the money to the treasury, used it to buy the potter's field in order to bury strangers. The Gospel account presents this as a fulfillment of prophecy.

Matthew 27:3-10 - "Then (as Jesus was being handed over to Pilate) Judas, who had betrayed him, saw that he was condemned and in his remorse returned the thirty silver coins to the chief priests and elders, with the words, "I was wrong - I have betrayed an innocent man to death." "And what has that got to do with us?" they replied. "That's your affair."

But the chief priests picked up the money and said, "It is not legal to put this into the Temple treasury. It is, after all, blood-money." So, after a further consultation, they purchased with it the Potter's Field to be a burial-ground for foreigners, which is why it is called "the Field of Blood" to this day.

---

[89] www.en.wikipedia.org/wiki/Judas Iscariot

And so the words of Jeremiah the prophet came true:

'And they took the thirty pieces of silver, the value of him who was priced, whom they of the children of Israel priced, and gave them for the potter's field, as the Lord directed them' (***Zechariah 11:12,13; Jeremiah 32:6-9)."***

"And Judas flung down the silver in the Temple and went outside and hanged himself". Acts 1:18-19 This man (Judas) had bought a piece of land with the proceeds of his infamy, but his body swelled up and his intestines burst. This fact became well known to all the residents of Jerusalem so that the piece of land came to be called in their (Aramaic) language Akeldama, which means "the field of blood"."

St. Paul[90]

St. Paul of Tarsus, also called **Paul the Apostle**, the **Apostle Paul**, or **Saint Paul**, (Ancient Greek: **Σαούλ (*Saul*), Σαῦλος** (*Saulos*), and **Παῦλος** (*Paulos*); Latin: *Paulus* or *Paullus*; Hebrew: **שאול התרסי *Šaul HaTarsi*** (*Saul of Tarsus*) was a Hellenistic Jew who called himself the "**Apostle to the Gentiles**" and was, together with Saint Peter and St. James the Just, the most notable of early Christian missionaries. According to the ***Acts of the Apostles***, his conversion took place on the road to Damascus. Thirteen epistles in the New Testament are attributed to St. Paul. The Epistles to the Thessalonians were written a decade before the remainder of the New Testament including the Gospels. His conversion experience is recorded in ***Acts*** and **1 *Corinthians***:

> **For what I received I passed on to you as of first importance that Christ died for our sins according to the Scriptures, that he was buried, that he was raised on the third day according to the Scriptures, and that he appeared to Peter and then to**

90 www.en.wikipedia.org/wiki/Judas Iscariot

the Twelve. After that, he appeared to more than five hundred of the brothers at the same time, most of whom are still living, though some have fallen asleep. Then he appeared to James, then to all the apostles, and last of all he appeared to me also, as to one abnormally born. For I am the least of the apostles and do not even deserve to be called an apostle, because I persecuted the church of God. But by the grace of God I am what I am, and his grace to me was not without effect. ***(1 Corinthians 15:3-10)***

St. Paul arrived in Jerusalem 57 *AD* with a collection of money for the congregation there. Acts reports that the church welcomed St. Paul gladly, but it was apparently a proposal of St. James that led to his arrest. St. Paul caused a stir when he appeared at the Temple, and he escaped being killed by the crowd by being taken into custody. He was held as a prisoner for two years in Caesarea until, in AD 59, a new governor reopened his case. He appealed to Caesar as a Roman citizen and was sent to Rome for trial. Acts reports that he was shipwrecked on Malta where he was met by St Publius (***Acts 28:7***) and the islanders, who showed him "unusual kindness."(***Acts 28:1***). He arrived in Rome *c* 60 *AD* and spent two years under house arrest.

Irenaeus of Lyons believed that St. Peter and St. Paul had been the founders of the Church in Rome and had appointed Linus as succeeding bishop. Though not considered a bishop of Rome, St. Paul is considered highly responsible for bringing the Christianity to Rome.

St. Paul traveled widely, made at least three major missionary journeys, wrote many letters of which thirteen still exist (some scholars dispute three of them), and his life and work is touched upon in a variety of ways in his letters. On returning to Jerusalem after his third journey, he was arrested and during his subsequent trials, as a Roman citizen "appealed to Caesar" for judgment - all covered by ***Acts 21-26. Chapters 27 and 28*** then describe St. Paul's voyage and journey to Rome in fascinating nautical detail. For some two years after his arrival in Rome, he was under house-arrest, before possibly being executed in the persecutions of Emperor Nero that followed the burning of Rome in 64 *AD*. However, most scholarship places his death later, possibly as late as 68 *AD*.

The apocryphal ***Acts of Paul*** comes from the second century. They describe St. Paul as "a man small of stature, with a bald head and crooked legs, in a good state of body, with eyebrows meeting and nose somewhat hooked, full of friendliness; for now he appeared like a man, and now he had the face of an angel!".

Tradition has said that Paul was beheaded, likely at Tre Fontane Abbey (English: Three Fountains Abbey) in Rome, and that the church of St. Paul stands over his grave). By comparison, St. Peter was crucified upside-down. This account fits with the report from Acts that St. Paul was a Roman citizen and would have been accorded the more merciful execution. St. Paul was executed by beheading (the merciful method of a privileged Roman citizenship) around the year 68 AD. St. Paul's relics are said to be located in St. Paul's Basilica, five miles from that of St. Peter. In his cell, prior to his execution, he wrote his last letter - the Second Letter to Timothy.

In the final analysis...

Twelve original Apostles were called personally by Jesus Christ. When Judas Iscariot hanged himself, the Christians nominated St. Matthias to complete the twelfth Apostolic position. St. Matthias is not mentioned in this treatise because the scriptures do not record his personal calling by Jesus Christ. Our resurrected Lord called one other Apostle, St. Paul, on the Damascus road.

The Apostles were empowered with the Holy Spirit after the Christ ascended. Prior to that time, they were disciples of Christ, not Apostles, and had no recorded empowerment. Most were simple fishermen or laborers of low estate. The exception was St. Paul who had rabbi credentials, could speak Greek, Hebrew, Aramaic and Latin fluently, and was educated “at the feet of Gameliel”, the foremost Pharisee teacher at the time.

The ***Acts of the Apostles*** details the missionary work of St. Paul and other Apostles, characterized by a great number of conversions and miracles, but also extreme opposition by the Jews, Greeks and Romans: They were arrested, flogged, severely beaten, imprisoned, shipwrecked, and almost all, with the probable exception of St. John, were eventually martyred.

A small band of simple, somewhat introverted men were transformed into the most powerful spiritual force the world has ever known. St. Paul, a Roman citizen, a sworn Jewish enemy of the Christian “way”, was transformed into one of the most powerful Christian Evangelists. The Apostles preached the Gospel in the known world, performed miracles, healed the sick, raised the dead, transformed the poor in spirit, and exorcised the evil spirits.

Jesus said, “And these signs will accompany those who believe: In my name they will drive out demons...they will place their hands on sick people, and they will get well."(Mark 16:17-18) This same Spirit, the Holy Spirit of the Resurrected Lord, promises to enable us, as Christians, to be without fear... empowered... peaceful... thankful.. unto an everlasting Spiritual life with Him. Shalom.

Week 1, *Jesus Christ and His chosen Apostles**
Suggested Questions for Discussion:

1. Which of Jesus' chosen disciples did not become an Apostle and why? What is the difference between an Apostle and a disciple?

____

____

____

2. When were the Apostles empowered by the Holy Spirit? Do we witness that same empowerment today?

____

____

____

3. Which Apostle was called in a different way from the others? Why did he and others consider him an Apostle?

____

____

____

* Additional space is provided on the next page.

The End of the First Week

(Please jot down any additional notations which may be helpful in group discussions.)

THE LENTEN SERIES

Week 2

WHY JUDAISM WILL NOT ACCEPT CHRISTIANITY

Why does the majority of the Jewish world reject Jesus as the Messiah ? According to the Rabbi : [91] ,the Jews do not accept Jesus as the messiah because they believe:

1. **Jesus did not fulfill the messianic prophecies.**
2. **Jesus did not embody the personal qualifications of the Messiah.**
3. **Biblical verses "referring" to Jesus are mistranslations.**
4. **Jewish belief is based on national revelation.**
5. **Christianity contradicts Jewish theology.**

.

1) "Jesus did not fulfill the Messianic prophecies"

What is the Messiah supposed to accomplish? The Bible says that He will:

- Build the Third Temple (Ezekiel 37:26-28).
- Gather all Jews back to the Land of Israel (Isaiah 43:5-6).
- Usher in an era of world peace, and end all hatred, oppression, suffering and disease. As it says: "Nation shall not lift up sword against nation, neither shall man learn war anymore." (Isaiah 2:4)
- Spread universal knowledge of the God of Israel, which will unite humanity as one. As it says: "God will be King over all

[91] www.simpletoremember.com/articles/a/jewsandjesus/

the world -- on that day, God will be One and His Name will be One" (Zechariah 14:9).

- The historical fact is that Jesus fulfilled none of these messianic prophecies.

Christians counter that Jesus fulfilled some prophecies and will fulfill the remainder in scriptures in the Second Coming. For the Jews, no concept of a "second coming "exists.

2) "Jesus did not embody the personal qualifications of Messiah"

"Jesus was not a prophet".

- Prophecy can only exist in Israel when the land is inhabited by a majority of world Jewry. During the time of Ezra (circa 300 BCE), when the majority of Jews refused to move from Babylon to Israel, prophecy ended upon the death of the last prophets -- Haggai, Zechariah and Malachi.
- Jesus appeared on the scene approximately 350 years after prophecy had ended.

Christians counter that Jesus prophesied a great many things including minute details of His own death and resurrection. Therefore, the "death of prophecy" as the Jews refer, is not factual.

"Jesus was not a descendent of David".

- The Messiah must be descended **on his father's side** from King David (see Genesis 49:10 and Isaiah 11:1)
- According to the Christian claim that Jesus was the product of a virgin birth, he had no father -- and thus could not have possibly fulfilled the messianic requirement of being descended on his father's side from King David!

The Gospel of St. Luke's genealogy (Gentile perspective), traces the natural line, the genealogy from Adam to Jesus. It does indicate Joseph as the father of Jesus and adds the words, As was supposed. The Gospel of St. Matthew's genealogy (Jewish perspective), traces the royal line, the genealogy from Abraham to Jesus, again through Joseph as the father of Jesus. The exact words are "And Jacob begat Joseph the husband of Mary, of whom was born Jesus, who is called the Christ".

Joseph was the actual "stepfather" of Jesus if the virgin birth is considered, and Joseph's lineage of both the St. Luke and St. Matthew accounts, was through King David. There are some differences in the two genealogies. Under Jewish law, the son or legal son-in-law by marriage could be the rightful descendent. (i.e. Since females were never mentioned in genealogies, Mary, the daughter of Heli, in the Davidic line, was replaced in the genealogy by her legal husband, Joseph, in the St. Luke Gospel account.)

In Genesis 49:10, the scripture "the scepter shall not depart from Judah" does not stipulate that the Messiah will descend from the father's side, either naturally or royally. In Isaiah 11:1, "a rod out of the stem of Jesse" does not indicate all descendants on the father's side, either. It is written that Jesus Christ (named the Messiah in the Hebrew bible) came from the lineage of Judah (Philippians 2:10, Psalms 72:1-14) and specifically from David (2 Samuel 5:1-8).

"Jesus did not fulfill the Torah".

- The Messiah will lead the Jewish people to full Torah observance. The Torah states that all mitzvot remain binding forever, and anyone coming to change the Torah is immediately identified as a false prophet. (Deut. 13:1-4)

- Throughout the New Testament, Jesus contradicts the Torah and states that its commandments are no longer applicable. (see John 1:45 and 9:16, Acts 3:22 and 7:37)

Christians counter that Jesus said that "He came to fulfill all the Law and the prophets". It is recorded that He spent time in the synagogue when he was only 12 years of age teaching the Rabbis. Jesus was a scholar of the Hebrew bible. Rather than change the Torah, he simplified the message. For instance He proclaimed that the Jews give the 10 commandments...He gave only two commandments, Love your God and Love your neighbor as yourself.

<u>3) "Biblical verses referring to Jesus are mistranslations"</u>

"Mary, the mother of Jesus, was not a virgin"

- The Christian idea of a virgin birth is derived from the verse in Isaiah 7:14 describing an "alma" as giving birth. The word "alma" has always meant a young woman, but Christian theologians came centuries later and translated it as "virgin."
- This accords Jesus' birth with the first century pagan idea of mortals being impregnated by gods.

In the author's view, this seeming contradiction in terms may be the only plausible Jewish argument to the Christian message as written in scripture. In the Hebrew bible, the word for virgin occurs only twice. The word for "young maid or woman" occurs over 50 times. Isaiah 7:14 does indeed have the word for "young maid or woman" rather than the word for "virgin". It is apparent that the Septuagint may have mistranslated the virgin birth of Jesus.

Having said that, the Christians counter with two possibilities: 1) It is possible that in this case, the Jews meant virgin when they called Mary a young maiden, who, most probably in Jewish culture, was a virgin. 2) The Christian core message in the Gospel of atonement through the passion on the Cross and the Resurrection remains the same regardless of the virgin birth which is peripheral to the core message of salvation through the Messiah.

"The crucifixion was mistranslated".

- The verse in Psalms 22:17 reads: "Like a lion, they are at my hands and feet." The Hebrew word ki-ari (like a lion) is grammatically similar to the word "gouged."
- Christianity reads the verse as a reference to crucifixion: "They pierced my hands and feet."

Christians counter that the crucifixion of the Messiah, Jesus Christ, was prophesied and reported in excruciating detail. Psalms 22:17 specifically prophesies, "...they have pierced my hands and my feet". Using the Hebrew bible interpretation, "Gouged, they are at my hands and feet" seems to indicate the same and is self-explanatory.

"Isaiah chapter 53 does not refer to Jesus, as the "suffering servant."

- In actuality, Isaiah 53 directly follows the theme of chapter 52, describing the exile and redemption of the Jewish people.
- The prophecies are written in the singular form because the Jews ("Israel") are regarded as one unit.
- The Torah is filled with examples of the Jewish nation referred to with a pronoun.
- Ironically, Isaiah's prophecies of persecution refer in part to the 11th century when Jews were tortured and killed by Crusaders who acted in the name of Jesus.

- St. Gregory, 4th century Bishop of Nanianzus, wrote: "A little jargon is all that is necessary to impose on the people. The less they comprehend, the more they admire."

Christians counter that Isaiah 52 and 53 do indeed, have the theme of the suffering servant. The Messiah is the entire focus of the redemption of the Jewish people. This now becomes a matter of the Jews "having eyes but cannot see, ears but cannot hear".

4) "Jewish belief is based upon national revelation"

"Jewish belief is based solely on national revelation" (i.e. Cannot be revealed individually)

- Of the 15,000 religions in human history, only Judaism bases its belief on national revelation -- i.e. God speaking to the entire nation
- Judaism is not miracles. It is the personal eyewitness experience of every man, woman and child, standing at Mount Sinai 3,300 years ago
- . If God is going to start a religion, it makes sense He'll tell everyone, not just one person.

This Jewish argument is false given the history of the Jewish nation as written in the Hebrew bible. Christians counter the obvious: God revealed himself INDIVIDUALLY through the patriarchs, Abraham, Isaac and Jacob, and continued that individual revelation through Moses and the prophets Isaiah, Jeremiah, Ezekiel, Daniel and a number of minor prophets. These individual revelations were ultimately received by the "obstinate and thick-necked" nation of Israel very negatively and it was only through plagues, exile, and extended captivity that a remnant of the Jewish nation believed at all.

The Godly appearances and prophesies traditionally are through His chosen prophets alone to be revealed to the nation of Israel...and the world. Again, it is a matter of the Jews "having eyes but cannot see, ears but cannot hear".

5) "Christianity contradicts Jewish Theology"

"God is one God, not three".

- The Catholic idea of Trinity breaks God into three separate beings: The Father, the Son and the Holy Ghost (Matthew 28:19).
- Contrast this to the Shema, the basis of Jewish belief: "Hear O Israel, the Lord our God, the Lord is ONE" (Deut. 6:4). Jews declare the Shema every day, while writing it on doorposts (Mezuzah), and binding it to the hand and head (Tefillin). This statement of God's One-ness is the first words a Jewish child is taught to say, and the last words uttered before a Jew dies.
- In Jewish law, worship of a three-part god is considered idolatry -- one of the three cardinal sins that a Jew should rather give up his life than transgress. This explains why during the Inquisitions and throughout history, Jews gave up their lives rather than convert.
- Further, the Ten Commandments state: "You shall have no other gods BEFORE ME," meaning that it is forbidden to set up a mediator between God and man. (see Maimonides - Laws of Idolatry ch. 1)

Christians counter that the basis for the Christian religion is faith and belief in God, the Father, God the Son, and God the Holy Spirit... a Oneness in Spirit. Contrast the "oneness" with the Jewish scriptures on holy matrimony in which the man and wife

are said to be "one" even though they are two people. Similarly to the Trinitarian concept, three persons can become "one" in spirit....Three persons but one substance.

"Man is God?"

- Maimonides devotes most of the "Guide for the Perplexed" to the fundamental idea that God is incorporeal, meaning that He assumes no physical form. God is Eternal, above time. He is Infinite, beyond space. He cannot be born, and cannot die. Saying that God assumes human form makes God small, diminishing both His unity and His divinity. As the Torah says: "God is not a mortal" (Numbers 23:19).

- Judaism says that the Messiah will be born of human parents, and possess normal physical attributes like other people. He will not be a demi-god, and will not possess supernatural qualities. In fact, an individual is alive in every generation with the capacity to step into the role of the Messiah. (see Maimonides - Laws of Kings 11:3)

This concept "oneness" is perhaps one of the most difficult to refute or reason. How is God eternal and yet finite in the human form of Jesus the Christ? Some Christians believe that Jesus was a partial manifestation of God on earth to communicate with humans more fully as an example and human leader. This somewhat divided deity concept is, of course, heretical in mainline Christendom as evidenced by the Nicene Creed in 325 AD. The Christ was also on earth as an atonement, a sacrifice to God, for the collective sins of mankind. Mainline Christians therefore reason that if Jesus Christ was a partial manifestation of God, why would a sacrificial atonement of Jesus (God's partial

manifestation) be necessary to sacrifice to God (fully manifested) ? It is perhaps the theological mystery of the ages for both Jew and Christian.

Christians believe that God came down to earth in human form, as Jesus said: "I and the Father are one" (John 10:30). Christians similarly to Numbers 23:19 also believe that God is not a mortal. When Jesus came to earth in human form as an example and "the Way" for all mankind, he did not relinquish His divinity or His "oneness" with God, the Father.

In the Final Analysis...

The Bible teaches that Jesus Christ was a Jew. In that sense, the Jews were the "chosen people". Indeed, the Bible relates many stories of the "stiff- necked and obstinate" Jews against the worship of the one true God. Not unlike any other race, the people turned their back on God. Many Jews would argue that it was the Romans who actually killed Jesus. The Bible teaches us that the Sanhedrin, the Jews, caused the trial and forced the eventual crucifixion of Jesus by selecting Barabbas to go free over Jesus at the trial.

What are we to say about the Jews? Were their questions brought forth valid enough to shed doubt on the Christ as the Jewish Messiah? They say that the Christian concept of the Trinity violates their monotheistic God. *The Trinity is indeed a concept which is difficult for most humans to fully grasp, including the Jews. God is one substance (i.e. Monotheistic) but three persons.* The non-fulfillment of the Messianic prophecies could simply be an error in the finite timetable according to the Jews, not an error in the Messianic timetable according to God almighty say the Christians. The Jewish unbelief of prophetic utterances of Christ was due to a "death of prophesy after Malachi" overstatement and misinterpretation of scripture.

The Jewish interpretation that the Messiah must be descended **on his father's side** from King David as stated in Genesis 49:10 and Isaiah 11:1 is incorrect. Neither scripture states "father's side". Joseph was of the lineage of David. If the Jews discount Joseph as the father due to the immaculate conception of Mary, it is written that Mary was the daughter of Heli in the Davidic line. Finally, the word for *young maiden* rather *virgin* appears to be in Isaiah 7:4. *Young maidens, particularly in Judaism, were most probably virgins with almost no exceptions.* Therefore, the so-called "mistranslation" may be of no real consequence.

The bible appears to be clear on one concept: Anyone (Jew, or Gentile) who does not believe that the Lord Jesus Christ came to save them (sinners), and, through that belief, becomes a practicing Christian in "thought, word and deed", will be lost. Not "chosen". **For God so loved the world that He gave His only begotten Son, that whoever believes in Him should not perish but have everlasting life"** (John 3:16). **Jesus answered, "I am the way and the truth and the life. No one comes to the Father except through me. If you really knew me, you would know my Father as well. From now on, you do know him and have seen him (**said to his Apostles**)."** (John 14:6-7).

Week 2, *Why Judaism will not accept Christianity**
Suggested Questions for Discussion:

1. Historically, did the Jews or the Romans crucify Jesus? Why is this relatively important or unimportant?

___

___

___

2. If the Jews did not understand the concept of the resurrected Christ, what clues in their ancient history would undergird this continued lack of understanding?

___

___

___

3. Contrast the New Testament versus the Old Testament concept of the "Messiah". Are they similar?

___

___

___

* Additional space is provided on the next page.

The End of the Second Week

(Please jot down any additional notations which may be helpful in group discussions.)

THE LENTEN SERIES

Week 3

UNDERSTANDING ISLAM

Muhammad ibn ‘Abdullāh (Arabicمحمد; *Muḥammad),* also spelled **Muhammed** or **Mohammed**) (ca. 570/571 – June 8, 632), was the founder of the religion of Islam and is regarded by Muslims as a messenger and prophet of God (Arabic**:** الله *Allāh*), the greatest law-bearer in a series of Islamic prophets, and, by most Muslims, the last prophet as taught by the Qur'an 33:40–40. Al-Masjid al-Nabawi (the Mosque of the Prophet) in Medina, Saudi Arabia, is the site of Muhammad's tomb. Muhammad was born approximately 534 years after Christ’s crucifixion and resurrection. The Hebrew bible and the New Testament had been written and translated into most of the world’s languages and dialects including the Arab world centuries before Muhammad came to power.

The Koran (English pronunciation: *kor-AHN*; Arabic: **القرآن** *al-qur’ān*, literally “the recitation”) is the religious text of Islam, also sometimes transliterated as Quran, Kuran, Koran, Qur’ān, Coran or al-Qur’ān. Muslims believe the Qur’an to be the verbal, divine guidance and moral direction for mankind. Muslims also consider the original Arabic verbal text to be the final revelation of God. The Koran is primarily attributed to Mohammed’s revelation from Allah through the angel Gabriel over a period of 23 years beginning in 610 C.E. It’s 144 chapters (or suras), include arab history, religious meaning and personal requirements for each Muslim follower of Allah. The reader is referred to the excellent website[92] for an online copy of the electronic version of The Holy Qur'an,

[92] www.uod.lib.umich.edu/k/koran/

translated by M.H. Shakir and published by Tahrike Tarsile Qur'an, Inc., in 1983.

The Old and New Testament biblical themes in the Koran are repetitive: The references to the story of Abraham (Arabic: **Ibrahim**) – 70 times; The references to the story of Moses (Abrabic: **Musa**) – 143 times; The references to the story of Jesus (Arabic**: Isa son of Marium**) – 27 times. The references to the story of Lot (Arabic**: Lut)** and Sodom and Gomorrah (Arabic: **Ad and Samood**) – 27 times; The references to the story of Noah and the flood (Arabic: **Nuh**) – 45 times.

He also mentions the stories of Adam, Aaron (Arabic: **Haroun**), Ramses (Arabic: **Firon**), Joseph (Arabic: **Yusef**), Zacharia (Arabic: **Zikiriah**), David (Arabic: **Daswood**), Solomon (Arabic: **Solaiman**), Ishmael (Arabic: **Ismael**), Isaac (Arabic: **Ishaq**), Jacob (Arabic**: Yaquob**) and others many times in the Koran. All of these persons are considered prophets/apostles with Mohammed (Arabic: **Muhammad**) mentioned as the last and main prophet and apostle of Allah. He is mentioned by name only 6 times, but mentioned as 'Allah and His Apostle' 69 times. **None of Jesus' apostles, miracles or resurrection appearances are mentioned or acknowledged in the Koran.**

Mohammed chose Ishmael, the son of the banished handmaiden of Abraham, rather than Isaac, as the chosen one of Allah (and the Arabic nation). The exact scripture from the Torah is as follows:

But Sarah saw that the son whom Hagar the Egyptian had borne to Abraham was mocking, and she said to Abraham, "Get rid of that slave woman and her son, for that slave woman's son will never share in the inheritance with my son Isaac. The matter distressed Abraham greatly because it concerned his son. But God said to him, "Do not be so distressed about the boy and your maidservant. Listen to whatever Sarah tells you, because it is through Isaac that your offspring [will be reckoned. I will make the son of the maidservant into a nation also, because he is your offspring." <u>Genesis 21:9-13.</u>

In his early years, Muhammed wrote of Jesus the Christ (Arabic: **Isa, son of Marium**) and revered him, as a prophet and apostle of Allah. Exact quotations from the Koran are as follows:

Second chapter of the Koran, **2. The Cow**, verse 62 following:

"Surely those who believe, and those who are Jews, and the Christians, and the Sabians, whoever believes in Allah and the Last day and does good, they shall have their reward from their Lord, and there is no fear for them, nor shall they grieve".

"And the Jews say: The Christians do not follow anything (good) and the Christians say: The Jews do not follow anything (good) while they recite the (same) Book. Even thus say those who have no knowledge, like to what they say; so Allah shall judge between them on the day of resurrection in what they differ".

.

Third chapter of the Koran, **3. The Family of Imran**, verse 53 following:

"When the angels said: O Marium, surely Allah gives you good news with a Word from Him (of one) whose name is the '. Messiah, Isa son of Marium, worthy of regard in this world and the hereafter and of those who are made near (to Allah).She said: My Lord! when shall there be a son (born) to I me, and man has not touched me? And (make him) an apostle to the children of Israel":

"That I have come to you with a sign from your Lord, that I determine for you out of dust like the form of a bird, then I breathe into it and it becomes a bird with Allah's permission and I heal the blind and the leprous, and bring the dead to life with Allah's permission and I inform you of what you should eat and what you should store in your houses; most surely there is a sign in this for you, if you are believers".

"And when Allah said: O Isa, I am going to terminate the period of your stay (on earth) and cause you to ascend unto Me and purify you of those who disbelieve and make those who follow you above those who disbelieve to the day of resurrection; then to Me shall be your return, so I will decide between you concerning that in which you differed. Surely the likeness of Isa is with Allah as the likeness of Adam; He created him from dust, then said to him, Be, and he was. Then Allah will say: O Isa son of Marium.

“Remember My favor on you and on your mother, when I strengthened you with the holy Spirit, you spoke to the people in the cradle and I when of old age, and when I taught you the Book and the wisdom and the Taurat and the Injeel; “

<u>Fourth chapter of the Koran, **4. The Women**, verse 172 following:</u>

“O followers of the Book! do not exceed the limits in your religion, and do not speak (lies) against Allah, but (speak) the truth; the Messiah, Isa son of Marium is only an apostle of Allah and His Word which He communicated to Marium and a spirit from Him; believe therefore in Allah and His apostles, and say not, “

“Three. Desist, it is better for you; Allah is only one God; far be It from His glory that He should have a son, whatever is in the heavens and whatever is in the earth is His, and Allah is sufficient for a Protector. “

<u>Fifth chapter of the Koran, **5. Dinner Table,** verse 73 following:</u>

“And with those who say, We are Christians, We made a covenant, but they neglected a portion of what they were reminded of, therefore We excited among them enmity and hatred to the day of resurrection; and Allah will inform them of what they did“.

“Certainly they disbelieve who say: Surely, Allah-- He is the Messiah, son of Marium. Say: Who then could control anything as against Allah when He wished to destroy the Messiah son of Marium and his mother and all those on the earth? And Allah's is the kingdom of the heavens and the earth and what is between them; He creates what He pleases; and Allah has power over all things“,

“O you who believe! do not take the Jews and the Christians for friends; they are friends of each other; and whoever amongst you takes them for a friend, then surely he is one of them; surely Allah does not guide the unjust people“.

“Certainly they disbelieve who say: Surely Allah is the third (person) of the three; and there is no god but the one God, and if they desist not from what they say, a painful chastisement shall befall those among them who disbelieve“.

“The Messiah, son of Marium is but an apostle; apostles before him have indeed passed away; and his mother was a truthful woman; they both used to eat food.Those who disbelieved from among the children of Israel were cursed by the tongue of Dawood and Isa, son of Marium; this was because they disobeyed and used to exceed the limit. “

Ninth chapter of the Koran, **9. The Immunity,** verse 30 following:

“And the Jews say: Uzair (Ezra) is the son of Allah; and the Christians say: The Messiah is the son of Allah; these are the words of their mouths; they imitate the saying of those who disbelieved before; may Allah **destroy** them; how they are turned away! “

Nineteenth chapter of the Koran, **19. Marium,** verse 147 following:

“And mention Marium in the Book. So she took a veil (to screen herself) from them; then We sent to her Our spirit, and there appeared to her a well-made man. He said: I am only a messenger of your Lord: That I will give you a pure boy. She said: When shall I have a boy and no mortal has yet touched me, nor have I been unchaste? He said: Even so; your Lord says: It is easy to Me: “

“and that We may make him a sign to men and a mercy from Us, and it is a matter which has been decreed.And the throes (of childbirth) compelled her to betake herself to the trunk of a palm tree.Then (the child) called out to her from beneath her: Grieve not, surely your Lord has made a stream to flow beneath you; And shake towards you the trunk of the palmtree, it will drop on you fresh ripe dates:Such is Isa, son of Marium; (this is) the saying of truth about which they dispute“.

"He (Jesus) said: Surely I am a servant of Allah; He has given me the Book and made me a prophet; And He has made me blessed wherever I may be, and He has enjoined on me prayer and poor-rate so long as I live; And dutiful to my mother, and He has not made me insolent, unblessed; And peace on me on the day I was born, and on the day I die, and on the day I am raised to life. Such is Isa, son of Marium; (this is) the saying of truth about which they dispute".

The Five Pillars of Islam (Sunni)[93]

Shahadah is a statement professing monotheism and accepting Muhammad as God's messenger. The *shahadah* is a set statement normally recited in Arabic: *(ašhadu an) lā ilāha illá l-Lāhi wa (ashhadu 'anna) Muḥammadan rasūlu l-Lāhi* "(I profess that) there is no god but Allah and Muhammad is the messenger of God."

Salah is the daily prayer of Islam. *Salah* consists of five prayers: *Fajr*, *Dhuhr*, *Asr*, *Maghrib*, and *Isha'a*. Fajr is said at dawn, Dhuhr is a noon prayer, Asr is said in the afternoon, Maghrib is the sunset prayer, and Isha'a is the evening prayer. All of these prayers are recited while facing Mecca. Muslims must wash themselves before prayer. They must also face Mecca when they pray

Zakāt or alms-giving is the practice of charitable giving by Muslims based on accumulated wealth, and is obligatory for all who are able to do so. It is considered to be a personal responsibility for Muslims to ease economic hardship for others and eliminate inequality. Zakat consists of spending 2.5% of one's wealth for the benefit of the poor or needy, including slaves, debtors and travelers.

---

93 www.en.wikipedia.org/wiki/Five_Pillars

Three types of fasting (**Sawm**) are recognized by the Qur'an: Ritual fasting, fasting as compensation for repentance (both from sura Al-Baqara), and ascetic fasting (from Al-Ahzab) Ritual fasting is an obligatory act during the month of Ramadan. Muslims must abstain from food, drink, and sexual intercourse from dawn to dusk during this month, and are to be especially mindful of other sins.

The **Hajj** is a pilgrimage that occurs during the Islamic month of Dhu al-Hijjah to the holy city of Mecca, and derives from an ancient Arab practice. Every able-bodied Muslim is obliged to make the pilgrimage to Mecca at least once in their lifetime if he or she can afford it. When the pilgrim is around 10 km (6.2 mi) from Mecca, he must dress in Ihram clothing, which consists of two white sheets.

In Shia Islam, the five pillars are more abstract and inward oriented:

1. Tawhid (monotheism)
2. Qiyamah (Day of Judgment)
3. Nubuwwah (Prophethood [prophets of Islam, Isa (Jesus), Jewish prophets, and other prophets])
4. Imamah (Leadership of the Twelve Imams)
5. Adl (Justice).

Outward profession of religion, although significant and crucial, do not count as pillars of faith in Shia Islam. A believer in the mentioned five pillars of Islam would believe in God, reward and punishment in the afterlife, the teachings of Muhammad and the prophets before him, in the leadership of the Twelve Imams, and in being just in thought, word, and action, which would entail adherence to outward profession of religiosity as defined in the Sunni five pillars of Islam.

Comparison of "Abrahamic Religions"

	Islam	Judaism	Christianitv
current adherents	1.7 billion	14 million	2.1 billion
major concentration	Middle East, Southeast Asia	Israel, Europe, USA	Europe, North and South America, rapid growth in Africa
sacred text	Qur'an (Koran)	Hebrew Bible	Hebrew Bible, New Testament
major splits	Shia/Sunni, c. 650 CE	Reform/Orthodox, 1800s CE	Catholic/Orthodox, 1054 CE; Catholic/Protestant, 1500s CE
main day of worship	Friday	Saturday	Sunday
identity of Jesus	true prophet of God, whose message has been corrupted	false prophet	Son of God, God incarnate, savior of the world
birth of Jesus	virgin birth	normal birth	virgin birth
death of Jesus	did not die, but ascended into heaven during crucifixion	death by crucifixion	death by crucifixion

Comparison of "Abrahamic Religions (con't)"

	Islam	Judaism	Christianitv
human nature	equal ability to do good or evil	two equal impulses, one good and one bad	"original sin" inherited from Adam – tendency towards evil
means of salvation	correct belief, good deeds Five Pillars	belief in God, good deeds	correct belief, faith, good deeds, sacraments (some Protestants emphasize faith
God's role in salvation	predestination	divine revelation and forgiveness	predestination, various forms of grace
resurrection of Jesus	(see above)	denied	affirmed

In the final analysis…

The Koran is a relatively small religious document compared to the much larger books of the Hebrew bible. Mohammed's interpretation of Allah's interaction with mankind through the re-telling of selected stories of the Old and New Testaments appears to be extremely repetitive. It is estimated that the Koran could be reduced by 2/3 of repetitive text regarding his retold versions of the biblical stories of Moses, Noah, Abraham, Joseph, Lot, David, Isaac, Jacob, Jesus and others…

- The overriding theme in the Koran is that "Allah is all powerful, beneficent and merciful". The religious doctrine is pure, albeit simple; the commands are to believe and worship Allah. Those who believe and worship Allah will go on to an eternal bliss in heaven (gardens with rivers flowing underneath). Those who do not believe and worship Allah will go on to an everlasting chastisement in a burning fire of hell and drink boiling water among other hideous things. It should be noted that the general concepts of belief, worship, heaven and hell are not unlike Judaism and Christianity.

- The proof of the existence of Allah in the Koran is His connection to mankind and the natural wonders in the world. The sun, the moon, the planets and stars all show Allah's greatness. All natural phenomena are a testament to Allah's omnipresence and omnipotence. The Koran incorporates Judaism's Torah, selected Psalms and a few selected portions of Christianity's history of Jesus to "prove" Allah's work through His prophets, primarily Mohammed. **Please contrast the eye-witness testimonies of the numerous miracles and the resurrection of Jesus Christ as the basis for Christianity. The "proof" and basis of the Islam faith was that Mohammed was a prophet as evidenced by his dictation of the Koran**.

- Major differences in Mohammed's version in the Koran and the Holy Bible exist. In the Koran, Ishmael is the chosen prophet of all peoples rather than the banished one of Judaism to the Arabic peoples. Rather than the resurrected Lord and savior in Christianity, Jesus is only a prophet in the Koran. It was noted that Jesus was crucified in the Koran; however, He ascended to Allah immediately. Unlike the other prophets in the Koran (including Mohammed), Jesus did not die and was never buried. Interesting...

Finally, it has been said by some in the western cultures that the Islam faith and the Koran represent a "**Jihad**", a holy war, against the "unbelievers". On the one hand, the Koran contains the words, "kill" ,"destroy", and "fight" 187 times. It basically teaches death and eternal torture to the unbeliever (i.e. *Infidel)*, On the other hand, the Koran teaches mercy, peace and compassion *for the Muslim believer.* It should be noted that the mainstream Muslim typically does not wage war. The Islam faith is basically a reverent faith, extolling the virtues of sobriety, moral behavior and charity. As in all religions, there appears to be an extreme, fundamentalist position shared by terrorists.

Allah is the one true God in the Islam faith, as is Yahweh in the Hebrew tradition. The God of the Christians embraces this one true God but we as Christians worship the one substance in three persons, God the Father, God the Son, and God the Holy Spirit. Although God has had many names throughout the centuries: Allah, Yahweh, Father, Jehovah, Elohim, Adonai, I AM, He is the one true God over all faiths and peoples.

This concept of "We kill" and the resurrected Lord are where Christianity emerges as the one true religion. Unlike all other religions, Jesus arose from the dead. He was passive (i.e. non-combative) toward his accusers in his life and crucifixion.

In the "day of resurrection", eternal life with the "Father" will be inherited by the faithful. Fiery Hell will be the eternally damned place of the proud, the "unbelievers." Jesus did not advocate that we kill our enemies. His command was to love... even as Christ (as God) loves us.

Week 3, *Understanding Islam**

Suggested Questions for Discussion:

1. What are the key differences between the story of Ishmael in the Hebrew bible and the Koran? Why is this important?

____

____

____

2. How does the authority of Mohammed differ from the authority of Jesus Christ as a founder of a religion? What are the dfferences between the Sunnis and Shias?

____

____

____

3. What are the similarities among the 3 Abrahamic religions: Judaism, Islam and Christianity?

____

____

____

* Additional space is provided on the next page.

The End of the Third Week

(Please jot down any additional notations which may be helpful in group discussions.)

THE LENTEN SERIES

Week 4

EASTERN RELIGIONS

Eastern religions refers to religions originating in the Eastern world — India, China, Japan and Southeast Asia —and thus having dissimilarities with Western religions. This includes the East sian and Indian religious traditions, as well as animistic indigenous religions. Religions originating on the Indian subcontinent include Hinduism, Buddhism, Jainism, and Sikhism. The theologies and philosophies of these religions have several concepts in common: D*harma*, K*arma*, *Maya* and *Samsara*.

Hinduism

Hinduism originated on the Indian subcontinent. **It is considered by some to be the world's oldest extant religion.** Hinduism contains a vast body of scripture, divided as revealed and remembered, expounding on dharma, or religious living. Hindus consider the *Vedas*and the *Upanishads* as being among the foremost in authority, importance and antiquity. The ***Bhagavad Gītā***, a treatise excerpted from the *Mahābhārata*, is sometimes called a summary of the spiritual teachings of the *Vedas*. It is difficult to identify any universal belief or practice in Hinduism, although prominent themes include: *Dharma*, *Samsara*, *Karma*, and *Moksha*. Hinduism is sometimes called a polytheistic, but this is an oversimplification. Hinduism includes a diverse collection of schools whose beliefs span monotheism, polytheism, pantheism, monism and even atheism.

Buddhism

Buddhism is a dharmic, non-deistic religion and philosophy. Buddhism was founded around the fifth century BCE in India by Siddhartha Gautama, the Buddha, with the Four Noble Truths and the Eightfold Path as its central principles. According to the scriptures, the Four Noble Truths were revealed by the Buddha in his first sermon after attaining enlightenment.

The **Four Noble Truths** (Sanskrit: *catvāri ryasatyāni*; Pali: *cattāri ariyasaccāni*) are one of the central teachings of the Buddhist tradition. The teachings on the four noble truths explain the nature of dukkha (Pali; commonly translated as "suffering", "anxiety", "stress", "unsatisfactoriness"), its causes, and how it can be overcome. According to the Buddhist tradition, the Buddha first taught the four noble truths in the very first teaching he gave after he attained enlightenment, as recorded in the discourse *Setting in Motion the Wheel of the Dharma (Dharmacakra Pravartana Sūtra)*, and he further clarified their meaning in many subsequent teachings. The four noble truths can be summarized as follows:

The truth of *dukkha* (suffering, anxiety, stress)
The truth of the origin of *dukkha*
The truth of the cessation of *dukkha*
The truth of the path leading to the cessation of *dukkha*

Jainism

Jainism is the religion of the followers of Mahavira. He is said to be the 24th Tirthankara, or the 24th in a line of teachers espousing Jain principles. Jains reject the Vedas and highlight the practice of austerity. Jain faith states that the jiva, or soul, can escape the cycle of rebirth and death through strict ethical behavior. When nothing remains but the purity of the jiva, that person is called a *jina*, or winner, which is the origin of the term Jain. Karma is viewed as an accumulation that burdens the soul, causing attachment and suffering. Ahimsa, or non-violence, is central to Jain faith and practice. It is interpreted very strictly as prohibiting all forms of harm to other living beings. Due to this, Jainism requires a strict vegetarian lifestyle. *Ahimsa* also applies to speaking, as one's words can cause harm and suffering.

Sikhism

Sikhism is a religion which began in Northern India. It is founded on the teachings of Guru Nanak Dev and the nine human gurus that followed. He received a vision to preach the way to enlightenment and God in Sultanpur. His views rejected the traditional worships and caste of the Hinduism faith. Freedom from reincarnation is tied to remembrance and repetition on one universal God. God is formless and simultaneously in every form. Sikhs believe that there is one universal God who is the ultimate creator, sustainer, and destroyer. The Gurū Granth Sāhib are the central scriptures intended to preserve hymns and the teachings of the Sikh Gurus and other saints from Hindu and Sufi traditions. Rituals, religious ceremonies or empty worship are considered of little use and Sikhs are discouraged from fasting or going on pilgrimages. The tenants of Sikhism include (1) honest living/earning (2) tithing and giving alms (3) chanting on God. Sikhism also has a strong warrior tradition which arose in defense of religious freedom and human rights from a tyrannical Moghul occupation of India.

Taoism

Taoism is a variety of related religious and philosophical traditions. Categorization of Taoist sects and movements is very controversial. Taoist propriety and ethics places an emphasis on the Three; love, moderation, humility. Taoist theology focuses on doctrines of wu wei ("non-action"), spontaneity, humanism, rrelativism and emptiness.

Most traditional Chinese Taoists are polytheistic. There are disagreements regarding the proper composition of this pantheon. Popular Taoism typically presents the Jade Emperor as the head deity. Intellectual, or "elite", Taoism usually presents Laozi and the Three Pure Ones at the top of the pantheon. Nature and ancestor spirits are common in popular Taoism. But this sort ofshamanism is eschewed for an emphasis on internal alchemy among the "elite" Taoists. Tao itself is rarely an object of worship, being treated more like the Central Asian concept of atman.

Shinto

Shinto is an animistic folk religion from Japan. Shinto literally means "the way of the gods". Many Japanese Shintoists also identify themselves as Buddhists. Japanese Pure Land Buddhism is deeply intertwined with the Shinto faith. Shinto practitioners commonly affirm tradition, family, nature, cleanliness and ritual observation as core values. Taoic influence is significant in their beliefs about nature and self-mastery.

Ritual cleanliness is a central part of Shinto life. Shrines have a significant place in Shintoism, reflecting the animistic veneration of the kami. "Folk", or Shinto places an emphasis on shamanism, "popular", particularly divination, spirit possession and faith healing. "Sect" Shinto is a diverse group including mountain-worshippers and Confucian Shintoists

Confucianism

Confucianism is a complex system of moral, social, political, and religious thought, influential in the history of East Asia. It is commonly associated with legalism but it rejects legalism for ritualism. It also endorses meritocracy as the ideal of nobility. Confucianism has a complicated system governing duties and etiquette in relationships. Confucian ethics focus on familial duty, loyalty and humaneness.

Confucianism tolerates the Chinese folk recognition of the existence of animistic spirits, ghosts and deities. It approves paying them proper respect, but at a more fundamental level encourages avoiding them. Confucian thought is notable as the framework upon which the syncretic Neo-Confucianism was built.

In the final analysis...

Eastern religions, particularly Hinduism, predated Abrahamic Judaist religion by at least 400-500 years. Most scholars will set the beginning time of Hinduism at the Aryan invasion in about 1800 BC. Most scholars would also agree that the beginning of oral tradition was in 1350 BC which culminated in the writing of the some parts of the Hebrew bible during the reign of King David in approximately 1100 BC.

Eastern religions were polytheistic; that is, they worshipped many gods, usually taking the form of animals, reptiles or natural objects or occurrences. It is difficult to identify any universal belief or practice in most of the religions although Hinduism does focus all the gods upon one supreme being. There are parallels of this teaching to the monotheistic one true God of the Judaist, Islam and Christian faiths.

Buddhism focuses on the four truths. Using the baseline truth of *dukkha* (suffering, anxiety, stress) and the understanding thereof, the remaining truths are defining the origin, the cessation, and the path leading to the cessation of suffering, anxiety and stress. Again, there are parallels of this teaching to the Christian message of faith and trust in Jesus Christ which leads to cessation of anxiety and stress. Christ also teaches that He brings peace in the midst of suffering although He concedes that we must all go through suffering even as He suffered on the cross for our souls.

Most eastern religions teach incarnation which is not found in Christian doctrine. Much the opposite, the Christian message is that each of us must once-and-for-all believe in the Lord and Savior *in our lifetime* or be banished (i.e. Separated) from God. We do not have the choice of coming back to life in various forms to renew our quest for the truth, wisdom or knowledge until we get it "right".

This Eastern doctrine paralleled the Gnostic heresy of the Christian church during the first few centuries. The Gnostics (i.e. Greek word for

Wisdom) were a large group in the early church who called themselves *Christian.* They maintained that each of us has a "divine spark of wisdom" which some called 'the God spark". As we grew in wisdom, the divine spark grew until we were all knowing and similar to God. This heresy was very difficult to parse given that the Christian church teaches that each of us has the Holy Spirit within us and it teaches us discernment and wisdom as we grow in the Faith.

The difference between these two doctrines is the origination and presence of the divine spark. On the one hand, the eastern religions believe that the divine spark started with us and is part of us. We own it. The Christian message teaches that although the "divine spark" is within us as Christians, it is the Trinity (i.e. God the father, God the Son, and God the Holy Spirit), who is a separate force, substance and being from us which guides and advises us. Regardless of how much knowledge and wisdom we ultimately possess, we cannot elevate ourselves or become God or become equal to His son, or savior Jesus the Christ.

Week 4, *Eastern Religions**

Suggested Questions for Discussion:

1. What is the oldest religion on earth and how is it basically different than the most popular religion in terms of adherents, Christianity?

___

___

___

2. Do the Eastern religions worship a Deity, and, if not, what do they worship or hold sacred? What is the role of suffering in the Eastern religions?

___

___

___

3. Describe the Eastern religion concept of Reincarnation and how that differs from the Christian concept of renewed life and afterlife in Christ.

___

___

___

* Additional space is provided on the next page.

The End of the Fourth Week

(Please jot down any additional notations which may be helpful in group discussions.)

THE LENTEN SERIES

Week 5

MAJOR RELIGIONS OF THE WORLD

A number of the major world religions[94] and their approximate # adherents, world percentage and a brief narrative of each of the religious beliefs are as follows:

Christianity

2.1 billion (33 %)

Christianity (from the Greek word **Χριστός,** ***Khristos,*** "Christ", literally "anointed one") is a monotheistic religion based on the life and teachings of Jesus of Nazareth as presented in the New Testament. Christianity is comprised of three major branches: Catholicism, Eastern Orthodoxy (which parted ways with Catholicism in 1054 A.D.) and Protestantism (which came into existence during the Protestant Reformation of the 16th century). Protestantism is further divided into smaller groups called denominations.

Christians believe that Jesus is the son of God, God having become man and the savior of humanity. Christians, therefore, commonly refer to Jesus as Christ or Messiah. Adherents of the Christian faith, known as Christians, believe that Jesus is the Messiah prophesied in the Hebrew Bible (the part of scripture common to Christianity and Judaism, and referred to as the "Old Testament" in Christianity).

---

94 www.en.wikipedia.org/wiki/Major_Religions

The foundation of Christian theology is expressed in the early Christian ecumenical creeds, which contain claims predominantly accepted by followers of the Christian faith. These professions state that Jesus suffered, died from crucifixion, was buried, and was resurrected from the dead to open heaven to those who believe in him and trust him for the remission of their sins (salvation). They further maintain that Jesus bodily ascended into heaven where he rules and reigns with God the Father. Most denominations teach that Jesus will return to judge all humans, living and dead, and grant eternal life to his followers. He is considered the model of a virtuous life, and both the revealer and physical incarnation of God. Christians call the message of Jesus Christ the Gospel ("good news") and hence refer to the earliest written accounts of his ministry as gospels.

Islam

1.5 billion (21 %)

Islam (Arabic: الإسلام *al-'islām,* is the monotheistic religion articulated by the Qur'an, a text considered by its adherents to be the verbatim word of the one, incomparable God (Arabic: الله, Allāh), and by the **Prophet of Islam Muhammad's teachings** and normative example (in Arabic called the Sunnah, demonstrated in collections of Hadith). *Islam* literally means "submission (to God)." ***Muslim***, the word for an adherent of Islam, is the active participle of the same verb of which *Islām* is the infinitive (see Islam (term)). Religious practices include the Five Pillars of Islam, which are five obligatory acts of worship. Islamic law (Arabic: شريعة) touches on virtually every aspect of life and society, encompassing everything from banking and warfare to welfare and the environment.

The majority of Muslims belong to one of two denominations, the Sunni and the Shi'a. Islam is the predominant religion in the Middle East, North Africa, and large parts of Asia and Sub-Saharan Africa. Sizable communities are also found in China and Russia, and parts of the Caribbean.

Islam's fundamental theological concept is ***tawhīd***—the belief that there is only one god. The Arabic term for God is *Allāh*; most scholars believe it was derived from a contraction of the words *al-* (the) and *ʾilāh* (deity, masculine form), meaning "the god" (***al-ilāh***), but others trace its origin to the Aramaic *Alāhā*. Other non-Arabic nations might use different names, for instance in Turkey the Turkish word for God, "Tanrı" is used as much as Allah.

The **Qur'an** is divided into 114 suras, or chapters, which combined, contain 6,236 *āyāt*, or verses. The chronologically earlier suras, revealed at Mecca, are primarily concerned with ethical and spiritual topics. The later Medinan suras mostly discuss social and moral issues relevant to the Muslim community. The Qur'an is more concerned with moral guidance than legal instruction, and is considered the "sourcebook of Islamic principles and values"

Hinduism

900 million (14 %)

Hinduism is the predominant and indigenous religious tradition of South Asia. Hinduism is often referred to as ***Sanātana Dharma*** (a Sanskrit phrase meaning "the eternal law") by its adherents. Generic "types" of Hinduism that attempt to accommodate a variety of complex views span folk and Vedic Hinduism to bhakti tradition, as in Vaishnavism. Hinduism also includes yogic traditions and a wide spectrum of "daily morality" based on the notion of karma and societal norms such as Hindu marriage customs.

Hinduism is formed of diverse traditions and has no single founder. Among its roots is the historical Vedic religion of Iron Age India, and as such Hinduism is often called the "**oldest living religion**" or the "oldest living major tradition". Demographically, Hinduism is the world's third largest religion, after Christianity and

Islam, with approximately one billion adherents, of whom approximately 828 million live in the Republic of India.

A large body of texts is classified as Hindu, divided into **Śruti** ("revealed") and **Smriti** ("remembered") texts. These texts discuss theology, philosophy and mythology, and provide information on the practice of **dharma** (religious living). Among these texts, the ***Vedas*** are the foremost in authority, importance and antiquity. Other major scriptures include the *Upanishads*, *Purāṇas* and the epics *Mahābhārata* and *Rāmāyaṇa*. The *Bhagavad Gītā*, a treatise from the *Mahābhārata*, spoken by Krishna, is of special importance.

Hinduism as we know it can be subdivided into a number of major currents. Of the historical division into six darshanas, only two schools, Vedanta and Yoga survive. The main divisions of Hinduism today are Vaishnavism, Shaivism, Smartism and Shaktism. Hinduism also recognizes numerous divine beings subordinate to the Supreme Being or regards them as lower manifestations of it. Other notable characteristics include a belief in reincarnation and karma, as well as in personal duty, or dharma.

Chinese traditional religion

394 million (6 %)

Chinese folk religion (also named **Folk Taoism** or **Shenism**) is a collective label given to various folkloric beliefs that draw heavily from Chinese mythology. It comprises the religion practiced in much of China for thousands of years, which included ancestor worship and drew heavily upon concepts and beings within Chinese mythology. Chinese folk religion is sometimes seen as a constituent part of Chinese traditional religion, but more often, the two are regarded as synonymous. It is estimated that there are at least 394 million adherents to Chinese folk religion worldwide.

Ceremonies, veneration, legends, festivals and various devotions associated with different folk gods/deities and goddesses form an important part of Chinese culture today. The veneration of secondary gods does not conflict with an individual's chosen religion, but is accepted as a complementary adjunct to Buddhism, Confucianism or Taoism. Some mythical figures in folk culture have been integrated into Buddhism, as in the case of ***Miao Shan***. She is generally thought to have influenced the beliefs about the Buddhist ***bodhisattva Kuan Yin.*** This bodhisattva originally was based upon the Indian counterpart Avalokiteshvara. Androgynous in India, this bodhisattva over centuries became a female figure in China and Japan. Kuan Yin is one of the most popular bodishisattvas to which people pray. Other folk deities may date back to pre-Buddhist eras of Chinese history. The Chinese dragon is one of the key religious icons in these beliefs. The absence of a proper name for this religion has for a long time caused Chinese folk religion to be viewed by Westerners as a popularized version of an "authentic" religion. Both in China and elsewhere, adherents often describe themselves, or are described by others, as followers of Buddhism, Taoism, Confucianism, or a mix among these.

Buddhism

376 million (6 %)

Buddhism is a religion and philosophy encompassing a variety of traditions, beliefs and practices, largely based on teachings attributed to Siddhartha Gautama, commonly known as the Buddha (**Pāli/Sanskrit "the awakened one")**. The Buddha lived and taught in the northeastern Indian subcontinent sometime between the 6th and 4th centuries BCE. He is recognized by adherents as an awakened teacher who shared his insights to help sentient beings end suffering (or **dukkha**), achieve nirvana, and escape what is seen as a cycle of suffering and rebirth.

Two major branches of Buddhism are recognized: **Theravada ("The School of the Elders") and Mahayana ("The Great Vehicle").** Theravada—the oldest surviving branch—has a widespread following in Sri Lanka and Southeast Asia, and Mahayana is found throughout East Asia and includes the traditions of Pure Land, Zen, Nichiren Buddhism, Tibetan Buddhism, Shingon, Tendai and Shinnyo-en. In some classifications Vajrayana, a subcategory of Mahayana, is recognized as a third branch. While Buddhism remains most popular within Asia, both branches are now found throughout the world. Various sources put the number of Buddhists in the world at between 230 million and 500 million, making it the **world's fourth-largest religion**.

The foundations of Buddhist tradition and practice are the Three Jewels: the Buddha, the Dharma (the teachings), and the Sangha (the community). Taking "refuge in the triple gem" has traditionally been a declaration and commitment to being on the Buddhist path and in general distinguishes a Buddhist from a non-Buddhist. Other practices may include following ethical precepts, support of the monastic community, living and becoming a monastic, meditation (this category includes mindfulness), cultivation of higher wisdom and discernment, study of scriptures, devotional practices, ceremonies, and invocation of buddhas.

Judaism

14 million (.2 %)

Judaism is the "religion, philosophy, and way of life" of the Jewish people. Originating in the Hebrew Bible, also known as the **Tanakh**, and explored in later texts such as the **Talmud**, Jews consider Judaism to be the expression of the covenantal relationship God developed with the Children of Israel. According to traditional **Rabbinic Judaism**, God revealed his laws and commandments to Moses on Mount Sinai in the form of both the Written and Oral Torah.0 This was historically challenged by the Karaites who maintain that only the Written Torah was revealed, and, in modern times, liberal movements such as Humanistic Judaism may be nontheistic. Judaism claims a historical continuity spanning more than 3000 years. It is one of the oldest monotheistic religions, and the oldest to survive into the present day. Its texts, traditions and values have inspired later Abrahamic religions, including Christianity, Islam and the Baha'i Faith. Many aspects of Judaism have also directly or indirectly influenced secular Western ethics and civil law.

Jews are an ethno religious group that includes those born Jewish and converts to Judaism. In 2007, the world Jewish population was estimated at 14 million, of whom about 40% reside in Israel and 40% in the United States. The largest Jewish religious movements are **Orthodox Judaism, Conservative Judaism and Reform Judaism.** A major source of difference between these groups is their approach to Jewish law.

Nonreligious/Agnostic/Atheist

1 Billion (21.7 %)

Atheism, in a broad sense, is the rejection of belief in the deities. In a narrower sense, atheism is specifically the position that there are no deities. Most inclusively, atheism is simply the absence of belief that any deities exist.

Week 5, *Summary: Major Religions of the World**

Suggested Questions for Discussion:

1. Which religion is gaining more adherents in recent history and what is the attraction for this religion?

___

___

___

2. Describe and contrast each major religious belief in one sentence.

___

___

___

3. Most religions have ***concentrations*** along geographical boundaries. True or false. Discuss the concept of a one world religion. Is this prophecied in any of the religious documents?

___

___

___

* Additional space is provided on the next page.

The End of the Fifth Week

(Please jot down any additional notations which may be helpful in group discussions.)